BETHLEHEM ROAD

Books by Michael Whitworth

The Epic of God
The Derision of Heaven
Living & Longing for the Lord
Esau's Doom

BETHLEHEM ROAD

A GUIDE TO RUTH

Michael Whitworth

START2FINISHBooks
A trusted, engaging guide to God's Word.

ISBN-10: 098851219X
ISBN-13: 978-0988512191

Library of Congress Control Number: 2014944445

Published by Start2Finish Books
PO Box 680, Bowie, Texas 76230
www.start2finishbooks.com

Printed in the United States of America

Cover Design: Josh Feit, Evangela.com

To my mother, who met the death of her husband
with an unflinching faith in the providence of God.

I will love you forever.

CONTENTS

FOREWORD

Nothing can prepare you for the death of your child. When my daughter, Ashley, died of cancer at age fourteen, my heart broke irreparably in two. My world collapsed. The future seemed dark. Hope appeared dashed against the jagged rocks of despair. I didn't want to be comforted, nor was I very interested in finding peace. I just wanted to hurt.

What are you supposed to do when joy and hope are swallowed up in grief—when darkness pierces your soul and seems to destroy every possible chance of happiness, or hope, or light—and you can't even muster up enough strength to care? Where are you supposed to turn? How do you reconnect with some sense of purpose and promise for your life? Or *can* you? Is there any hope left?

The Bethlehem Road can be a dismal journey. When the struggles of life become unbearable, the only path some can find actually leads them away from God, away from hope, away from the only source of genuine peace. Some never find their way back and spend the rest of their lives lost in a spiritual fog, void of any purpose or direction. But the Bethlehem Road runs both ways. As certainly as it can lead one away from peace and hope and God, it can also provide the path home.

In *Bethlehem Road*, Michael Whitworth masterfully weaves together the spiritual and pragmatic implications of the story of Ruth and Naomi. He takes us behind the curtain to see the historical and cultural context in which this age-old story unfolds. He brings together a wide array of scholarship and adds his own unique insights as he explores the story's various details.

Most important, he makes sure we don't miss the connection between this ancient story and our modern lives: God is ever-present on the Bethlehem Road, even when we cannot see him or feel his guiding hand. He is patient when the road takes us away from him, and he is waiting to redeem us when the road brings us back.

God's redemption. That's what this story is really all about. Sure, there are the very human elements of struggle, sacrifice, love, friendship, and faithfulness. Yes, the romantic component is epic, inspiring the music of countless weddings. It's undeniable that tragedy and heartache play major roles in the story's development and the direction of the main characters' lives.

But at the final curtain call, it is God's faithfulness that takes the bow. Only God is big enough to restore hope in the midst of utter despair. Only he can redeem the mourner's grief and grow something beautiful out of the dark soil of emotional and spiritual destitution. Only God can work all things together—even the bad things, even the darkest of days—to produce something good (Rom 8:28).

Every Naomi needs a faithful Ruth. But ultimately, every Naomi needs to trust in the God of all hope to turn the Bethlehem Road into a journey of renewal. Having friends and loved ones who will stand beside us, hold our hands, and cradle our broken hearts is of immeasurable value. That's a valid and important take-away from this beautiful story. But only when we turn to God and collapse in his arms will we rediscover life, peace, and purpose in the midst of tragedy. Only then can hope be rekindled.

So remember this: Dark days will come. Laughter will turn into mourning. Life will fall apart all around you. And when it does, God is the One who can redeem your heartache. Hold on to his hand as tightly as you can, and don't ever let go.

— Paul O'Rear, Author of
Living With a Broken Heart

INTRODUCTION

W hat do you do when your dreams are shattered?

In 1985, I was born to a preacher and his wife in Morton, Mississippi. From birth, I was a daddy's boy. We often went on road trips together and threw the football in the backyard. Dad was a passionate gospel preacher, and he taught me everything I know about preaching and ministry. But more than a great father and a good preacher, Dad was my best friend. Every week of college, he and I shared a meal together and talked about life. We were headed for a lifetime of rich friendship that only a father and son can know.

Then, on September 16, 2004, a little after noon, a college professor and close family friend summoned me to his office. With a distraught look on his face, he sat me down, wrapped his arm around my shoulder, and told me my father had died. All at once, I lost a dad, mentor, and friend.

What do you do when your dreams are shattered?

What do you do when your spouse of five, ten, or thirty years says, "I don't love you anymore"? What do you do when you realize "happily ever after" will never characterize your marriage?

What do you do when you realize you and your spouse will never have children—that late-night feedings, T-ball practices, and toys on Christmas morning aren't in your future?

What do you do when you realize the company you've served

faithfully for so many decades is laying you off—only a few months shy of retirement?

What do you do when you realize your child is never coming home again—never repenting of rebellion—and that holidays, vacations, and family reunions will never be the same?

What do you do when you suffer loss upon loss upon loss until you're convinced that God is out to get you?

This book, the one you hold in your hands, is about the book of Ruth. Many Christians already know Ruth's story. It is a short story (just four chapters) that tells of Ruth's unselfish devotion to her mother-in-law, Naomi. It is a beautiful story with a romantic theme, complete with a knight coming to rescue the damsel in distress. The book of Ruth "runs the full range of human emotions, from the most gut-wrenching kind of grief to the very height of glad-hearted triumph."[1] It even has a twist in the end that you never see coming—a note about Ruth's famous great-grandson, David. But the story of Ruth really isn't about Ruth or Naomi or Boaz or even David. Nor is it a story about pain or suffering or loss.

A lot of theories have been put forth as to why the book of Ruth was written.[2] Was it to encourage levirate obligations or to support the assimilation of Gentiles into Israel? Was it intended to be a defense of mixed marriages? A celebration of faithful lovingkindness in times of need? A polemic on the importance of women in a male-dominated society?

On one level, the book of Ruth may serve as a defense of David's legitimate claim to Israel's throne.[3] Remember that David ruled only over Judah at first; Israel wasn't united under him for the first seven years. Moreover, a lot of foreigners enjoyed positions of influence in David's administration, and I'm sure his political enemies tried to slander him as

---

1.   John MacArthur, *Twelve Extraordinary Women* (Nashville: Nelson, 2005), 69.

2.   Katrina J. A. Larkin, *Ruth and Esther* (Sheffield: Sheffield Academic, 2000): 52–56. "Attempts to specify a single purpose falter in light of the book's richness and complexity," (Phyllis Trible, "Ruth, Book of," ABD 5:846).

3.   Kirsten Nielsen, *Ruth* (Louisville: Westminster John Knox, 1997), 21–28.

an illegitimate usurper since his great-grandmother had been a Moabite. If you think about it, it's not that different from those who question President Obama's birth certificate. So Ruth's story may have been meant to affirm that, although she was a Moabite, she had been a faithful servant of God and a virtuous member of the Bethlehem community. Ruth exemplified how "foreigners who adopt Yahweh and outdo the Israelites in *hesed* merit acceptance as full-fledged Israelites."[4]

But even this goal seems secondary to a grander purpose. Ruth's story is about God and his faithfulness to us when we hurt; it's about what God does when our dreams are shattered; it's about discovering God's providence in the midst of our pain, even in the smallest, most insignificant decisions of life.[5] Ruth's great-grandson would find solace in this very promise: "Even when I walk through the darkest valley, I will not be afraid, for you are close beside me" (Ps 23:4 NLT).

The narrator of Ruth's story doesn't spend a lot of time on death and grief; rather, the focus is on Naomi's return to Bethlehem, to her family, to Israel… to God. After only five verses, we find Naomi on the road back to Bethlehem. So this story—and the book you hold in your hands—is about traveling that daunting Bethlehem Road.

We're often told that life is a journey—one with many forks in the road. But no matter what path we choose, every road becomes broken somewhere along the way. The smooth pavement eventually gives way to a twisted path of bad decisions and shattered dreams. The Bethlehem Road even traverses the frightening valley of the shadow of death at times. When Dad died, I started walking this road, and life hasn't been the same since. John Piper reminds us that:

---

4.   Robert L. Hubbard, *The Book of Ruth* (Grand Rapids: Eerdmans, 1988), 45. "Ruth firmly insists that true belonging to the people of YHWH cannot be by physical descent only," (Philip Satterthwaite and Gordon McConville, *Exploring the Old Testament: A Guide to the Historical Books* [Downers Grove, IL: InterVarsity Press, 2007], 229).

5.   "This book highlights how God's people experience his sovereignty, wisdom, and covenant kindness. These often come disguised in hard circumstances and are mediated through the kindness of others," (*ESV Study Bible* [Wheaton, IL: Crossway, 2008], 475).

The life of the godly is not an Interstate through Nebraska but a state road through the Blue Ridge Mountains of Tennessee. There are rockslides and precipices and dark mists and bears and slippery curves and hairpin turns that make you go backward in order to go forward. But all along this hazardous, twisted road that doesn't let you see very far ahead, there are frequent signs that say, "The best is yet to come." Taken as a whole, the story of Ruth is one of those signs. It was written to give us encouragement and hope that all the perplexing turns in our lives are going somewhere good. They do not lead off a cliff. In all the setbacks of our lives as believers, God is plotting for our joy.[6]

You should know that nothing uniquely qualifies me to write this book. I'm not a counselor or therapist. I've never so much as attended a workshop or seminar on grief counseling. I'm not a psychologist, psychiatrist, or doctor (though I sometimes play one on television!).

But I know what it's like to have your world crash down around you. I know what it's like to believe you will never smile or laugh again, to believe that heaven has betrayed you, to believe that you have been abandoned, forsaken, and left alone. I know what it's like to be so adrift in the ocean of grief and self-pity that you lose the will to keep on living. I know what it's like to drive down deserted country highways at night, looking for a tree to wrap your car around.

I know how despondent and despairing the Bethlehem Road can be.

I also know that, despite what we might think or feel, God never forsakes us on the Bethlehem Road. His *silence* does not equate to his *absence*. Naomi thought God was against her, but the book of Ruth proves that this was not the case. What's interesting is that God proved Naomi wrong, yet he didn't do so through a prophet, priest, or king. There is

---

6.   John Piper, *A Sweet and Bitter Providence* (Wheaton, IL: Crossway, 2010), 99–100.

no divine revelation in the story of Ruth, nor are there any spectacular miracles, but God was at work nonetheless.

This book doesn't provide a 12-step plan to anything. This book does not promise to deliver you from suffering, disappointment, or tragedy. In fact, reading this book might dredge up a wellspring of emotions you thought you had long buried in the deep recesses of your heart. Studying and reflecting on God's Word has a way of doing that.

What I *can* promise you is that this book will remind you of how powerful and merciful God is, of how fiercely he loves you, and of how he has adored you since before the foundation of the world. What I hope is that this book will leave you in awe of the Lord's ability to redeem the worst events for our good and his glory. If you've been living with a broken heart—if bitterness and disappointment have been your travel companions on life's journey—then Ruth's story will inspire and strengthen you as you travel the Bethlehem Road.

More than anything, I pray this book will bring you to your knees in worship of your Redeemer and King.

RUTH Q&A

In a recent interview with myself, I asked some questions about this guide to Ruth. I hope the answers orient you to this guide and to this marvelous story.

Q: Who wrote Ruth?

A: We don't know, as the book is anonymous. Jewish rabbis in the Talmud claimed Samuel was the author (*Baba Bathra* 14b), but this is unlikely, since the prophet died before David achieved enough political and historical notoriety to merit mention at the end of the book. A plausible alternative is the prophet Nathan.[1] If you want to get technical, God authored Ruth because his Spirit inspired its composition (2 Pet 1:21).

Q: When was Ruth written?

A: Since we don't know who wrote it, we cannot date the book definitively. A considerable amount of time must have passed between Ruth's lifetime and the story's composition, indicated by the explanatory note in 4:7. Years ago, most scholars believed the book was penned sometime after the Babylonian exile, perhaps in the days of Ezra and

---

1. Joyce Baldwin, "Ruth" in *New Bible Commentary*, 4th ed. (Downers Grove, IL: InterVarsity Press, 1994), 287.

Nehemiah. These scholars argue that the book of Ruth contains several
Aramaic phrases that would date it to the 6th or 5th centuries B.C.,[2]
just as words like "Internet," "email," and "HDTV" would date a book
to our own time. However, such a late date for Ruth is now considered
untenable for several reasons. For one thing, the OT prophets had a
rather negative impression of Moabites, whereas Ruth, a Moabite, is
positively portrayed in this story. Moreover, both Ezra and Nehemiah
considered mixed marriages to be a religious faux pas (Ezra 10:1–17;
Neh 13:1, 23), while the narrator of Ruth seems ambivalent. More
recent scholarship has favored a pre-exilic date. Harrison points out
that it would have been difficult for a latter author, no matter how
talented, to recapture the milieu of Judges.[3] This means that Ruth was
written closer to, but no earlier than, 1000 B.C., when David reigned
(cf. 4:17, 22) and friendly relations existed between Israel and Moab
(1 Sam 22:3). Archer, in agreement with Harrison, reasonably argues
that, had the book of Ruth been written after Solomon, his name
would have been included in the genealogy at the book's end.[4] As his
name does not appear, it can be assumed that Ruth was written after
1000 B.C. and before Solomon became king in 970 B.C.

Q: Do we at least know when the story of Ruth takes place?

A: All the book tells us is that its events took place during the period
of the book of Judges (c. 1300–1050 B.C.). Jewish sources variously
date the book to the very end of the Judges period, but also as early

---

2. Contra Driver: "The general Hebrew style (the idioms and the syntax) shows no marks
of deterioration; it is palpably different, not merely from that of Esther and Chronicles, but even from
Nehemiah's memoirs or Jonah, and stands on a level with the best parts of Samuel," (S. R. Driver, *An
Introduction to the Literature of the Old Testament*, Rev. ed. [New York: Scribner's, 1914], 454).

3. R. K. Harrison, *Introduction to the Old Testament* (Grand Rapids: Eerdmans, 1969),
1061–62.

4. Gleason L. Archer, Jr., *A Survey of Old Testament Introduction*, Rev. ed. (Chicago: Moody,
1974), 280. For a brief, but very good, overview of the debate as to when Ruth was written, see A.
Graeme Auld, *Joshua, Judges, and Ruth* (Philadelphia: Westminster Press, 1984) 259.

as the time of Ibzan (also of Bethlehem), whom the rabbis identified as Boaz.[5] Some scholars connect the story to the time of Gideon (c. 1190 B.C.), but this may be a bit too early. Assuming there are no gaps in the genealogy between Obed and David, the story takes place later in the Judges period, arguably as late as Jephthah's day (c. 1075 B.C.). Regardless, as Block rightly states, "Any attempt to narrow the particular time of the events recorded in this book is speculative."[6]

Q: What can you tell us about Moab and the Moabites?

A: The nation was born out of the incestuous episode between a drunken Lot and his oldest daughter (Gen 19:37). Chemosh was the chief national deity of the Moabites (Num 21:29; Jer 48:46). They were perpetual enemies of Israel (e.g. Judg 3:12–30; 1 Sam 14:47; 2 Kgs 3:1–27), except for a few brief seasons of peace (as in Ruth's and David's lifetimes). While Israel was wandering in the wilderness, it was the king of Moab who hired Balaam (the one with the talking donkey) to curse Israel (Num 22–24). Later, the women of Moab led the men of Israel into sin; the story found in Num 25:1–9 is one I don't remember learning about in Sunday school as a kid. The Moabites' origin and antagonism towards Israel may explain why both Moab and Ammon (the other son born as a result of Lot's incest) were excluded from the congregation of the Lord (Deut 23:3). The rest of the OT does not depict Moab favorably (cf. Ps 60:8; Isa 15–16; Jer 48; Ezek 25:8–11; Amos 2:1–3). The stigma of being from Moab, rather than a member of God's chosen people, follows Ruth throughout the story; her ethnicity is mentioned in six different places (1:22; 2:2, 6, 21; 4:5, 10). But Ruth redeems this stigma, much as the Good Samaritan parable cast Samaritans in an unexpectedly positive light.[7]

---

5. Tamara Cohn Eskenazi and Tikva Frymer-Kensky, *Ruth* (Philadelphia: Jewish Publication Society, 2011), 4.

6. Daniel I. Block, *Judges, Ruth* (Nashville: B&H, 1999), 624.

7. Victor P. Hamilton, *Handbook on the Historical Books* (Grand Rapids: Baker, 2001), 187.

Q: You're pretty famous for your threats to people who don't read the *Introduction* to these guides. But I've already read it, so I can safely ask: is there anything you didn't mention there that you'd like to mention now?

A: One of the interesting things about the book of Ruth is its placement in the canon. In Jewish Bibles, it was categorized in the Writings section, coming just after Proverbs. In Christian Bibles, however, it appears between Judges and 1 Samuel, as it takes place during the time of Judges, but also has a connection to David. Ruth's location in the Jewish canon connects the book (cf. 3:11) with the virtuous woman of Prov 31:10–31, while its place in Christian Bibles offers up a light of hope during the moral darkness of Judges (especially compared to Judges' final five chapters). Finally, it was Jewish tradition to read the book of Ruth during Pentecost, which celebrates the giving of God's Law at Sinai. By reading Ruth's story, Israel was reminded that God's Law was intended to be a means of gracious provision in troubled times, rather than a legalistic social experiment.

Q: What would be the best way to use this guide?

A: I recommend a four-pass system of studying Ruth. For example, to get the most out of Ruth 2, I suggest you read: 1.) all of Ruth (only 85 verses), 2.) Ruth 2 again, 3.) chapter 2 in this guide, and 4.) Ruth 2 again. Reading the story multiple times will help cement it in your mind, and you will catch details you missed previously.

Q: Did you discover anything interesting about Ruth while writing this guide that you didn't know before?

A: I did—many times. One thing in particular is that out of the 85 verses in the book, 55 are dialogue. Since that is the narrator's main way of driving the narrative, pay attention to the speeches and conversations; you'll get a lot more out of the story.

Q: What can you tell us about how this guide came together?

A: As always, I wrestled with what to include vs. omit. Some scholarly debates are much ado about nothing, and sharing everything a commentator said can be more of a hindrance than a help. I wanted the reader to understand God's Word, so I tried to anticipate and answer common questions that arise from the text. Don't expect me to deal with every issue, because that would exhaust us all. Besides, I don't expect you always to agree with my conclusions. I do, however, expect you to study and reflect on your own; then, and only then, make an informed decision. I want this guide to resemble a friendly conversation about Ruth, albeit one-sided. Each chapter ends with a few "Talking Points," points of application I hope will provide good material for lessons or sermons and spark positive discussion in a class or small-group setting. In the end, I want everyone who reads this guide to be comforted by Ruth's message and, consequently, have a greater faith in the providence of God.

Q: Do you recommend a specific Bible translation?

A: No. This guide primarily uses the English Standard Version (ESV), but it always helps to read the Bible in more than one translation. I definitely recommend a good Study Bible.

Q: Would you like to add anything else before we wrap up?

A: If you see an abbreviation you don't recognize, remember that there is an *Abbreviations* page in the back. Other than that, I want to encourage the reader to remember that the book of Ruth isn't really about Ruth—she isn't the main character, and neither is Naomi or Boaz. They are all supporting roles, but God is the Hero and Protagonist at the center of the story, just as he should be in our personal stories. He should be the One we turn to in our grief and suffering, when we are feeling loss or pain, because everything is ultimately about him (Rom 11:36).

And so with faithful Ruth we pray
That bitter providence today
Tomorrow will taste very sweet,
And every famine that we meet
And every broken staff of bread
In death, will bring us life instead.

JOHN PIPER

1

FOR BETTER OR WORSE

The town of Morton in Scott County, Mississippi, is small and of seeming insignificance. Over the past thirty years, little has changed. The chicken plant has closed down, and the Dairy Queen across the street from my old neighborhood has been replaced by some other business, one that (sadly) doesn't offer its customers a delightful fudge-dipped ice cream cone. A town of only three thousand souls, travelers on nearby Interstate 20 wouldn't know it was there if not for the word "Morton" shaped by shrubs on an overpass' embankment.

Morton was where my parents lived and where my dad preached when I was born. In those days, a young man finishing up medical school in nearby Jackson began working weekends in Morton's ER. A Christian, he started attending the blonde-brick church across the street from the ER, the very church that my dad served. Tim and Dad became quick friends. My parents invited him to sleep in their guest room when he was in town, and Tim and Dad often went for walks in the morning. It wasn't long before Tim and his wife, Pam, moved their young family to Morton, where the friendship between our families only deepened.

Thirty years later, Tim and Pam Ashley remain the most faithful friends my family has ever known. In all my memories of loss and sadness, I can recall Tim and Pam standing beside us, holding our hands, helping us pick up the pieces of our shattered lives. Their faithfulness to us in times of trouble has been enormous. Particularly in the dark season following my dad's unexpected death, their presence in our lives was proof to me that God had not forsaken my family.

Long ago, Solomon wrote, "Many claim to have unfailing love, but a faithful person who can find?" (Prov 20:6 NIV). Faithfulness in relationships is becoming a relic of a bygone era. Too many people now seek the blessings of a relationship, but are unwilling to accept the cost or commitment. But every so often in life, you come across people who become more than acquaintances. They bring joy in the good times and comfort in the bad. Their remarkable faithfulness is like a light of hope in abject darkness. These are your true friends.

The story of Ruth begins with darkness and sadness and pain—and then gets worse. It narrates the experiences of a family attempting to survive a famine by moving to a new home in search of a secure future. But death comes knocking, leaving behind in its awful wake three graves and three widows unable to pick up the pieces of their shattered lives because some of the pieces are now missing.

The first chapter of Ruth's narrative is famous for the grand declaration Ruth makes to her mother-in-law (1:16–17). Her words are often recited in matrimonial vows and inscribed within wedding bands. Ruth's commitment is certainly worthy of being emulated in marriage, but her dedication is all the more striking because it was not socially expected. Ruth was under no obligation—legal, social, or otherwise—to Naomi, yet she believed in being faithful in her relationships, regardless of the circumstances, the cost, or the need. Whatever happened to Naomi, Ruth would remain at her side for better or worse.

It is always difficult to walk the Bethlehem Road, but it's impossible to finish the journey if we are made to walk it alone. In our pain and bitterness, we need someone who will be faithful to us. Moreover, we should be faithful to others who walk the road, for it is often through such friends that God ministers to our heavy hearts.

As I reflect on the tragic seasons of my own life, the pain has often been mitigated (and God's grace has been ministered) by the faithfulness of my family friends, Tim and Pam Ashley, and their children—Ty, Katy, and Amber. In a time when relationships are cheaply bought and carelessly discarded, their "for better or worse" faithfulness has been a light of hope in abject darkness. They are my Ruth, coming to my side when I am in need of companionship on the Bethlehem Road.

RUTH 1:1–5

I somehow expected Ruth's story to begin with a vague "Once upon a time, in a land far away…" opening that would rob it of any concrete historical context. The book of Ruth, one teeming with romance and redemption, seems at home in the land of make-believe—but it's no fairytale. The story is real, and the events in this book affect real lives, real families; the drama centers on real tragedy and heartache.

The original readers of this book would have found the opening line—"In the days when the judges ruled"—to be quite ominous. This was a dark period in Israel's history, "an era of frightful social and religious chaos."[1] For roughly 300 years after Joshua's death, Israel languished in the Promised Land as little more than a loose confederacy of tribes that could barely elicit a national consensus on anything. Their political instability was a product of their spiritual rebellion. In Judg 2:11–23, we're given a cookie-cutter description of the appalling cycle of disobedience, disaster, suffering, and oppression at the hands of neighboring despots. God would hear his people's cry for help, send a savior/deliverer/judge to rescue them, and stability would return to the land, until the cycle began all over again.

The final chapters of Judges especially underscore the period's moral bankruptcy and spiritual blackness.[2] Following the Samson narrative (Judg 13–16), two stories are told that I imagine have never been featured

---

1. Hubbard, *Book of Ruth*, 84.

2. Throughout his commentary, Michael Moore draws several comparisons between Ruth and Judges' final chapters ("Ruth" in *Joshua, Judges, Ruth* [Grand Rapids: Baker, 2012]).

in VBS curriculum. The first (Judg 17–18) is about a man named Micah who stole 1,100 silver shekels (equivalent to at least $15 million today) from his mother, recast the silver into an idol, and hired a Levite to serve as a household priest. Sometime later, Danites were relocating from southern to northern Canaan and raided the man's house in the process, stealing the idol and his priest. That this illegitimate priest was the grandson of Moses (Judg 18:30) makes the story only more depressing.

The second story (Judg 19–21) concerns a Levite and his concubine, who spent the night in Gibeah on their way home from Bethlehem. Since Motel 6 hadn't left the light on for them, they found lodging in the home of a hospitable stranger. In a scene eerily reminiscent of Sodom, a mob arrived at the front door, wanting to have a homosexual orgy with the Levite (Judg 19:22). Out of desperation, the Levite gave the mob his concubine instead, only to find the next morning that she had been ravaged and left for dead. Enraged, the Levite hacked her corpse into a dozen pieces, sent a piece to each of Israel's tribes, and demanded justice be served (Judg 19:29–30). When the tribe of Benjamin refused to punish Gibeah, civil war broke out, and Benjamin was almost exterminated.

The book of Judges ends with a simple, but important exclamation: "In those days there was no king in Israel. Everyone did what was right in his own eyes," (Judg 21:25). This verse immediately precedes the book of Ruth in the Christian canon. It is expressive of dark, lawless times that would only be relieved in 1 Samuel. "From all outward appearances, God's purposes for righteousness and glory in Israel were failing. But what the book of Ruth does for us is give us a glimpse into the hidden work of God during the worst of times."[3]

No matter how dark and bleak our own world may become, no situation is ever beyond God's ability to redeem it. What he requires, however, are willing participants in his epic drama—souls willing to be vessels or conduits of his providence, redemption, and unfailing love.

---

3. Piper, *Sweet and Bitter Providence*, 22–23.

W e are immediately introduced in Ruth to a man named Elimelech, his wife, Naomi, and their two sons, Mahlon and Chilion. They are later identified as "Ephrathites," a note likely designating them as belonging to a well-to-do or well-respected family.[4] During a time of famine, they left their home in Bethlehem, where there was no bread in the "house of bread."[5] A town normally known for its production of wheat, barley, olives, almonds, and grapes was no longer able to feed itself.

Famine was a terrible reality in ancient times, one that not only forced people to seek food elsewhere, but sometimes required them to mortgage their property (Neh 5:3). More so than other towns in Israel, Bethlehem "was particularly susceptible to the climate because there was no spring and it relied on cisterns to gather water."[6] A farmer in this region "lived so near subsistence level that one or two bad harvests brought him near to ruin."[7] In contrast, Moab (across the eastern bank of the Jordan), where Elimelech and his family moved, was

> well watered by winter rains, and the soil is porous enough to hold this moisture for cereal crops and pasturage for sheep and goats. Places where the soil is deeper and springs are available (especially along the wadis which cut into the plateau from the Dead Sea escarpment) support fruit trees and vineyards. Thus, despite its deficiencies, Moab is reasonably good agricultural land

---

4. "He thereby underscored the humiliating tragedy involved: the Vanderbilts have suddenly become poor sharecroppers," (Hubbard, *Book of Ruth*, 91). Ephrathah was another name for Bethlehem (Gen 48:7; Mic 5:2).

5. "They actually left the house of bread in the middle of a famine to go to the fields of Moab. A house denotes a warm environment, as opposed to a field, that lies open and unprotected. In biblical writings, the empty field is an image that often precedes tragedy," cf. Gen 4:8; Deut 21:2; 22:25 (Raphael B. Shuchat, "The Use of Symbolism and Hidden Messages in the Book of Ruth," *JBQ* 30 [2002]: 111–12).

6. John H. Walton, Victor H. Matthews, and Mark W. Chavalas, *The IVP Bible Background Commentary: Old Testament* (Downers Grove, IL: InterVarsity Press, 2000), 277.

7. John Gray, *Joshua, Judges, Ruth* (Grand Rapids: Eerdmans, 1986), 384.

and accordingly is strewn with ruins of settlements from ancient times.[8]

We are not told the cause or reason for this famine (e.g. too much/ little rain, plant disease, insects, war[9]), possibly because it was a regular occurrence in Canaan and not always a direct result of God's displeasure.[10] These events, however, occurred in the Judges period, and when considering the covenant curses given through Moses, it's safe to assume that this particular famine was due to Israel's rebellion.

> If after all this you will not listen to me ... I will break down your stubborn pride and make the sky above you like iron and the ground beneath you like bronze. Your strength will be spent in vain, because your soil will not yield its crops, nor will the trees of your land yield their fruit.
>
> Lev 26:18–20 NIV

> However, if you do not obey the LORD your God and do not carefully follow all his commands and decrees I am giving you today, all these curses will come on you and overtake you: ... The sky over your head will be bronze,

---

8.   J. Maxwell Miller, "Moab," ABD 4:883. Driesbach explains further, "Weather systems carrying moisture blow in to Israel from the Mediterranean Sea and continue on into Jordan. As these systems move inland, the elevation of the land generally increases (with the obvious exception of the Jordan Valley) until the Jordan plateau is reached. At times clouds carrying significant moisture pass over the hills of Israel, where Bethlehem is located, and are not forced to release their rain until reaching the higher elevations of the Jordan plateau, where Moab was located," (Jason Driesbach, "Ruth" in *Cornerstone Biblical Commentary*, vol. 3 [Carol Stream, IL: Tyndale House, 2012], 513). "In the dry year 1931-32 there was more rain in the S highlands of Moab than at Bethlehem," (R. B. Y. Scott, "Palestine, Climate of" in *The Interpreter's Dictionary of the Bible*, vol. 3 [Nashville: Abingdon, 1962], 622).

9.   cf. Gen 41:27; 1 Kgs 18:2; 2 Kgs 8:1; Isa 1:7; Amos 4:9–10; Acts 11:28.

10.   "Overall, the pattern of famine and plenty in the Levant is unpredictable," (Dale W. Manor, "Ruth" in *Zondervan Illustrated Bible Backgrounds Commentary: Old Testament*, vol. 2 [Grand Rapids: Zondervan, 2009], 245).

the ground beneath you iron. The LORD will turn the rain of your country into dust and powder; it will come down from the skies until you are destroyed.

Deut 28:15, 23–24 NIV

The "why" of the famine, however, isn't a concern for the narrator. Mentioning it simply reminds the reader of past famines in the lives of Abraham, Isaac, Jacob, and Joseph, and how God used those seasons of despair to craft a wondrous narrative of redemption and deliverance.[11] In other words, "famine" in Scripture—no matter its cause or reason—is often a signal that God is about to act in a mighty way for the good of his people and the glory of his own name.

The narrator provides no background to the famine, nor does he offer a moral or spiritual judgment of Elimelech's decision to move the family to Moab.[12] For their part, scholars are torn on the issue:

> Why go off to a country and people whose god Chemosh demanded human sacrifice? Why join a nation whose king Eglon had pressed Israel into servitude for eighteen years (Judg. 3:14)?[13]

> What is Elimelek to do? His own farm cannot feed his family, and presumably the famine affects everyone else in the area so they cannot simply bail him out.[14]

---

11. Nielsen (*Ruth*, 40–41) notes several links between the narratives of Genesis and Ruth.

12. "The family of Elimelech would have traveled north to the area of Jerusalem and then taken the Jerusalem to Jericho road to cross the Jordan at the fords by Jericho. From there the road east up to Heshbon would connect them to the north-south King's Highway leading through the region of Moab. Depending on where they settled, the trip would have been seventy to one hundred miles and would have taken about a week," (Walton, *Bible Background*, 277).

13. David Jackman, *Judges, Ruth* (Dallas: Word, 1991), 317.

14. John Goldingay, *Joshua, Judges, and Ruth for Everyone* (Louisville: Westminster John Knox, 2011), 163.

Certainly, we would expect a man whose name meant "God is king" to remain in the Promised Land and trust the Lord to provide.[15] But Elimelech, whether out of stubborn rebellion or end-of-the-rope desperation, opted for the more fruitful foreign fields of Moab. There he moved his family, and there he died.

The text actually says that Elimelech and his family went to Moab "to sojourn," which can mean a temporary stay (cf. Gen 21:34; 2 Kgs 8:1–2; Jer 44:14) but more often indicates a permanent residence (cf. Exod 6:4; 2 Sam 4:3; Jer 49:18, 33; Ezek 47:22–23)—"Elimelech is no weekend tourist."[16] Regardless of how long the family intended to live in Moab, they would not have received rights as full citizens (e.g. an immigrant in Israel couldn't own land) and would have faced serious social challenges. Their experience would not have been so different from the challenges immigrants in America face today.[17] These difficulties, however, would have paled in comparison to the greatest tragedy of all: an Israelite had left the Promised Land to seek a better life among the Gentiles. The narrator might not have considered this a *sinful* occasion, but it was most certainly a *sad* one.

In time, Mahlon and Chilion married local women and settled down. It is not until the end of the story that we learn it was Mahlon who married Ruth (4:10), and Chilion who married Orpah. These two couples presumably had every intention of putting down roots and raising their children in Moab, but this was not to be. After a decade of childless marriages, both brothers died. We are left with three widows, three graves, and countless questions.

Easily missed in English, but striking in Hebrew, is the narrator's depiction of Naomi's state in the wake of the death of her husband and

---

15. "Elimelech's departure for Moab may reflect his own doubts about the truth his name declared," (Block, *Ruth*, 625).

16. Moore, "Ruth," 309.

17. "[A sojourner] lives among people who are not his blood relatives, and thus he lacks the protection and the privileges which usually come from blood relationship and place of birth," (TDOT 2:443).

sons. At the graves of her two sons, Naomi isn't referred to by her name, but by the generic epithet "the woman" (1:5). "It is as though Naomi has lost not only her family, but even her own name. That is the symbolic end point of her descent into emptiness."[18]

Also, the narrator uses a Hebrew term that literally means "to be left over." This expression is one that "speaks of bereavement at the death of another and often refers to those who have survived the wrath and judgment of God."[19] "Left over" or "left behind" is exactly how many people feel when they lose loved ones. Their despondency robs them of their will to move on, to keep living. Like last night's leftovers brought home in a doggie bag, survivors feel like they're just waiting their turn to be thrown out into life's landfill. If there is ever a time when faithful friends are needed in life, it is on the Bethlehem Road when storm clouds hide the face of God.

The opening verses of Ruth leave us with many unanswered questions. Did Elimelech and his sons die from accidents or natural causes? Or was God angry with them? Did he, in his divine wrath, strike them down? If Elimelech had remained in Bethlehem, would he have died so soon? If Mahlon and Chilion had not married foreign brides or lingered in Moab, returning instead to the Promised Land, would their days have been longer and their quiver filled with arrows (cf. Ps 127:5)? We would love for the narrator to answer our questions and satisfy our curiosity, but he doesn't.

Life has a habit of leaving our most pressing, perplexing questions unanswered.

What we are left with is circumstantial evidence that suggests Elimelech and his sons died because of their disobedience, though this is

---

18. Barry G. Webb, *Five Festal Garments* (Downers Grove, IL: InterVarsity Press, 2000), 40. "Elimelech's family hovers precariously on the brink of extinction. And in Israel, there was no greater tragedy than for a family to cease to exist," (Hubbard, *Book of Ruth*, 96).

19. Block, *Ruth*, 627–28; cf. Lev 26:36, 39; Deut 4:27; 28:62; Ezek 6:12; 9:8; Zech 11:9.

never explicitly stated. Younger argues, "Even a cursory knowledge of the Deuteronomic blessings and curses and the general moral degeneracy of the period of the judges raises the interpretive expectations here."[20] In other words, reading Ruth against the background of Deuteronomy and Judges strongly suggests that Elimelech and his sons were struck down because of their unfaithfulness to the Law of Moses. Jewish rabbis unapologetically blamed Elimelech's death on his leaving the Promised Land; similarly, the sons' deaths were consequences of their marrying Moabite women and failing to return to Bethlehem (*Ruth Rabbah* 2.10; *Baba Bathra* 91a).[21]

The Law did not explicitly prohibit intermarriage with Moabites (Deut 7:3). Geisler makes the excellent observation that the prohibition against intermarriage was motivated by morals and holiness, not racism.[22] Deuteronomy even specified the rules for marrying a foreign POW who was willing to assimilate into Israel and make Yahweh her God (Deut 21:10–14). Moreover, Hubbard argues that Esther's example proves this prohibition "was apparently not considered valid in a foreign land,"[23] meaning Naomi's sons would have been free to marry whomever they chose. For these reasons, I think Smith's conclusion is fair: "If this passage is intended to be a protest against religious intermarriage it certainly is a mild one."[24]

Block, however, persuasively argues that the narrator negatively viewed Mahlon and Chilion's marriages to foreign women; the specific Hebrew phrase translated as "took...wives" (1:4) often describes illegitimate marriages.[25] Furthermore, Jewish rabbis of old were suspicious

---

20. K. Lawson Younger, Jr., *Judges and Ruth* (Grand Rapids: Zondervan, 2002), 413–14.

21. Other Jewish interpreters (e.g. Ibn Ezra, Radak) claimed that Ruth and Orpah were properly converted before the nuptials.

22. "That God sanctioned marriage with people of varying ethnic groups is clear from his blessing upon Rahab and Ruth, both of whom were brought into the bloodline of the Messiah by intermarriage with Jews, and both of whom were women of faith," (Norman Geisler, *Systematic Theology*, vol. 2 [Minneapolis: Bethany House, 2003], 454–55).

23. Hubbard, *Book of Ruth*, 93, n. 10.

24. James E. Smith, *The Books of History* (Joplin, MO: College Press, 1995), 214.

25. Block, *Ruth*, 628–29.

of two marriages, each lasting a full decade, that never produced children (cf. Deut 28:18). Thus, Younger hypothesizes, "The covenantal implications are clear: As Yahweh withheld the rain and thus produced the famine, so he withheld fertility, hence no children."[26]

In our own time, it's often impossible to judge whether negative events are punishment from God (cf. John 9:2–3). In fact, just as the story of Job affirms that the worst things can happen to the best people, the NT makes clear that suffering and tragedy are ways in which God makes us worthy of his kingdom (2 Thess 1:5). After all, Jesus said that the rain (or lack thereof, in this case) falls on the righteous and wicked alike (Matt 5:45).

Personally, I don't know what to think concerning Elimelech and his sons. The text doesn't tell us why they died, so any conclusions are conjecture at best (well-reasoned though they may be). In the OT, God sometimes took a person's life; at other times, a person died without any direct involvement from heaven. I agree with Sakenfeld, who reasonably deduces that "the narrator's lack of attention to any reason suggests that the answer to the question is not central to the meaning of the story."[27] In other words, the author does not linger on the causes of famine and death, because these three graves are only intended to establish Naomi as a tragic figure on the Bethlehem Road. The only definitive conclusion is "that godly people do experience unexpected tragedies, and sometimes in rapid succession."[28]

RUTH 1:6–18

Sometime after the death of her sons, Naomi heard "that the LORD had visited his people" (1:6). The Hebrew verb used is a special term in Scripture, meaning "to attend to, take note of, care for."[29] Just as God

---

26. Younger, *Ruth*, 417.

27. Katherine Doob Sakenfeld, *Ruth* (Louisville: John Knox, 1999), 21.

28. Smith, *Books of History*, 214.

29. NIDOTTE 3:657.

visited Sarah and Hannah in their barrenness (Gen 21:1; 1 Sam 2:21), and Israel in her slavery in Egypt (Gen 50:24–25; Exod 4:31; cf. Jer 29:10), he now visited his covenant people to provide them with food. As with Sarah and Hannah and Israel, God's visitation would be the beginning of something wonderful.

Having received confirmation that the famine had abated, Naomi made plans to return home to Bethlehem. To a casual observer, it does not seem that God's visitation was connected to Naomi any more than to the other faithful in Israel. I'm left wondering, however, about the "coincidence" of God's visitation and the end of the famine occurring in the midst of Naomi's deepest despondency. Yahweh was bringing more than food to his people; he was using the famine's end to beckon Naomi to return home to God's people.[30] The Lord knew that Naomi needed to be around God's people if she were to know God's peace during this turbulent time in her life.

There were limited options for a widow in ancient Israel. Widowed and childless, Naomi had no male relatives to care for her needs. Had she been a younger woman,[31] Naomi might have chosen from three alternatives.[32]

Return to her parents' home. This is the option Naomi encouraged Ruth and Orpah to pursue. A widow could return to the safety and refuge of her father's house and hope for another offer of marriage. But there

---

30. "The provision which is spoken of here is a covenanted provision, which Naomi is at present missing out on because she has forsaken the covenant community. Her return is a choice to identify with that community again. It is a return, not just to Bethlehem, but to Yahweh and Yahweh's people." (Webb, *Five Festal Garments*, 42).

31. "If she was married at fifteen years of age and had her sons by twenty, and they in turn were twenty when they married, and this event occurs at least ten years later, she would now be at least fifty years of age, a senior citizen in that context and certainly past menopause," (Block, *Ruth*, 636).

32. Younger, *Ruth*, 418; cf. Paula S. Hiebert, "'Whence Shall Help Come to Me?': The Biblical Widow" in *Gender and Difference in Ancient Israel* (Minneapolis: Fortress, 1989): 125–41; TDOT 1:289–90.

is no mention of this option being available to Naomi, which means her parents were already dead in all likelihood.

Remarry. Arnold reminds us that "marriage was the only source of stability and security for a woman in the ancient Near East."[33] Women of childbearing years could remarry after the death of their husband. But Naomi was likely beyond menopause. In a time when a woman's main value was her ability to bear children, and barrenness was considered reasonable grounds for divorce, men would look to younger widows as prospective wives, favoring those who could still birth an heir (cf. Deut 25:5–10).

Support herself by working. After my dad died, my mom courageously went back to college, earned her degree, and has since enjoyed a successful career as an elementary school teacher (she was Teacher of the Year in 2013—I could not have been prouder!). But this was obviously not an option in ancient times, especially for an older woman. Later in the story, we are told that it was Ruth, not Naomi, who gleaned in the fields, which was itself a mere step above actual begging.

None of these options were open to Naomi. Bereft of her husband and sons—"the worst fate that an Israelite woman might experience"[34] (cf. Isa 1:23; 10:2)—life promised Naomi a future in slavery, prostitution (cf. Amos 7:17), or death.[35] Several places in Scripture underscore the plight of the widow,[36] who "lost all social status and generally were also without political or economic status. They would equate to the homeless in our American society. Typically they had no male protector and were therefore

---

33. Bill T. Arnold and Bryan E. Beyer, *Encountering the Old Testament,* 2nd ed. (Grand Rapids: Baker, 2008), 188.

34. Younger, *Ruth,* 418. "From an investigation of the resources available to the biblical widow to supply her economic needs a grim picture emerges. A woman's economic well-being was directly related to her link with some male. Though a married woman may have owned some property in the form of her dowry, she could not have supported herself on that alone, if at all, when her husband died," (Hiebert, "'Whence Shall Help,'" 137).

35. Karel van der Toorn, "Female Prostitution in Payment of Vows in Ancient Israel," *JBL* 108 (1989): 193–205; Manor, "Ruth," 247.

36. Deut 25:5–10; 2 Sam 14:7; 1 Kgs 17:17–20; Luke 7:11–17; 1 Tim 5:4–5.

economically dependent on society at large."[37] At any other time in Israel's history, Naomi might have received community support. However, these events occurred during the Judges period, a time when faithfulness to the Law and sincere concern for others was at an all-time low. Naomi thus had no substantive guarantee of a bright future in Moab or Bethlehem.

Later, Naomi expressed the belief that "that the hand of the LORD has gone out against me" (1:13). Her words echo the author of Judges: "Whenever [Israel] marched out, the hand of the LORD was against them for harm, as the LORD had warned" (Judg 2:15; cf. Exod 9:3; Deut 2:15). Just as God's hand (a concept found about forty times in the OT) went out against Israel because of her disobedience, Naomi believed God was against her (cf. Job 6:4). It would have been better for Orpah and Ruth to distance themselves from the "cursed" Israelite widow.

> If you have lost your farm, your country, your extended family, your husband, and your sons, it may seem there is a curse on you. If you stay attached to these two girls, will you not lose them, too? Better to anticipate the curse. They have alternatives not open to her. They have Moabite families they can go back to.[38]

Naomi's blessing on Orpah and Ruth is intriguing. Although she blamed God for her circumstances, she wished for Yahweh to bless them. More specifically, Naomi wished that the Lord would "deal kindly" with them (1:8), a translation of the Hebrew *hesed*. This is a rich OT term, and a foundational one in the book of Ruth, occurring only three times (1:8; 2:20; 3:10), but always at a pivotal moment. Yet *hesed* has proven

---

37. Walton, *Bible Background*, 277. "[Orphans, widows, and the poor] had no rights, no legal personalities, or in some cases possibly restricted rights. They were almost outlaws. Anyone could oppress them without danger that legal connections might endanger his position," (F. Charles Fensham, "Widow, Orphan, and the Poor in Ancient Near Eastern Legal and Wisdom Literature," *JNES* 21 [1962]: 139).

38. Goldingay, *Ruth*, 165–66.

notorious to translate adequately into English. It is variously rendered throughout its 245 OT occurrences as "mercy," "lovingkindness," "grace," "faithfulness," and "unfailing love." It is characteristic of one's love for others and of God's love for his people. The majority of occurrences of *hesed* occur in Psalms, particularly those of lament and help. Consider Ps 94:17–18 as an example: "Unless the LORD had given me help, I would soon have dwelt in the silence of death. When I said, 'My foot is slipping,' your unfailing love [*hesed*], LORD, supported me."

There is an element of loyalty to the idea of *hesed*, as well as doing for others what they can't do for themselves. "It is an act that preserves or promotes life. It is intervention on behalf of someone suffering misfortune or distress."[39] Harrison declares *hesed* to be "the motivating force of the Sinai covenant,"[40] and Alec Motyer described it best as "combining the warmth of God's fellowship with the security of God's faithfulness."[41] So it is odd that Naomi wished for God's *hesed* to go with Orpah and Ruth, yet she expressed such bitterness against the Lord. Naomi believed God was great, and perhaps he was still good, just to everyone but Naomi's family. Although she was unaware of it, God's *hesed* was already at work to redeem Naomi's broken heart. God was not against this Bethlehem widow.

Naomi vehemently chastised Orpah and Ruth when they attempted to accompany her. To do so was a form of living suicide. Naomi wanted them to prosper, which would not happen as long as they remained with her—or so she thought. "Thus, Naomi made her most crucial point. If even God was after her, to follow her home was to court personal disaster. Her earlier tragedies—famine, exile, bereavement, childlessness—might be only the beginning."[42] She was particularly insistent that the two young

---

39. TDOT 5:51.

40. R. K. Harrison, "Ruth" in *Evangelical Commentary on the Bible* (Grand Rapids: Baker, 1989), 181.

41. Quoted in Jackman, *Ruth*, 320.

42. Hubbard, *Book of Ruth*, 113.

widows return to their "mother's house" (1:8) and await the day when they could start over with a new family.[43]

It is important not to demonize Orpah for her decision to return to her family. As mentioned previously, given the options open to her, this was the best and most reasonable alternative. The narrator, however, uses her decision to do the sensible thing as a literary device in order to further elevate Ruth as the heroine in the story. "Orpah pursues the natural course; Ruth is determined to swim upstream."[44] Both of these women had to choose, not between right and wrong or good and bad, but better and best.

After Orpah returned to her mother's house, she is never mentioned again in Scripture.[45] The text then says that "Ruth clung to" Naomi (1:14), the same Hebrew verb used in Gen 2:24, where it speaks of a husband clinging to his wife and becoming one flesh, and in Deuteronomy regarding Israel's attachment to Yahweh (Deut 4:4; 10:20; 11:22; 30:20). Ruth clung to Naomi because she was intent on being as faithful to her mother-in-law as she had been to her husband. Regardless of the circumstances, the cost, or the need, she would stay by Naomi's side for better or worse. Naomi, on the other hand, thought Ruth simply needed an extra push to follow Orpah, but she was wrong. Ruth's stubborn response is among the most beloved and well-known statements in all the OT, towering "as a majestic monument of faithfulness above the biblical landscape."[46]

---

43. "In its other appearances in the Old Testament (Gen 24:28; Song 3:4; 8:2) the mother's house has to do with preparations for marriage. This corresponds to the situation in both Mesopotamia and Egypt, where the mother was protector of the daughter and the one who advised and supervised in matters of love, marriage and sex. Therefore, Naomi's encouragement of the girls to return to their mother's home does not suggest seeking a place of legal protection, but rather a place that may provide a new family situation," (Walton, *Bible Background*, 277).

44. Block, *Ruth*, 638; cf. Hubbard, "One may understand Orpah; one must emulate Ruth," (*Book of Ruth*, 116).

45. Jewish tradition recorded some fantastic tales of what happened to Orpah, including her being raped and abused for forsaking Naomi. Other traditions claimed that David, Ruth's great-grandson, killed Goliath, whom the rabbis said was the great-grandson of Orpah (*Ruth Rabbah* 2.20).

46. Hubbard, *Book of Ruth*, 117.

> Do not urge me to leave you or to return from following
> you. For where you go I will go, and where you lodge I
> will lodge. Your people shall be my people, and your
> God my God. Where you die I will die, and there will I
> be buried. May the LORD do so to me and more also if
> anything but death parts me from you.
>
> Ruth 1:16–17

How beautiful these words are! They show Ruth's inner resilience and selflessness, but more importantly her love for Naomi. Ruth felt as if Naomi was pressuring her to abandon her mother-in-law, but as God swore never to forsake his people (Deut 31:6, 8), so Ruth swore never to abandon Naomi.

Three of Ruth's promises are particularly striking. First, she says, "Your people shall be my people." That was a tall order since immigrant widows, young or old, didn't have it easy in ancient times. People couldn't just pack up and move away then as we do today (trust me, I've moved to a new place eleven times in my life). "Such mobility was almost impossible for ancient peoples, firmly rooted in a patriarchal and patrilocal culture. A text at Nuzi tells of a man who totally disinherits two of his sons because they moved to another town!"[47] Ruth, however, was fully intent on becoming an adopted Israelite.

Notable, too, is her adoption of Israel's God as her Lord. Instead of continuing to serve the Moabite deities as Naomi had encouraged[48] (1:15), Ruth became a servant of Yahweh.

> The gods of Moab become a part of Ruth's discarded
> past. She leaves a country whose very origin sounds

---

47. William Sanford LaSor, David Allan Hubbard, and Frederic Wm. Bush, *Old Testament Survey* (Grand Rapids: Eerdmans, 1982), 114, n. 93.

48. It is troubling that Naomi spoke of Orpah returning to "her gods" (1:15). It's impossible to know if she meant the chief Moabite god, Chemosh, the entire Moabite pantheon, or simply the household gods of Orpah's family (Moore, "Ruth," 321).

like a smutty joke, whose gods demand the sacrifice of
the firstborn sons and the prostitution of the daughters,
and goes to Israel, where the fertility has been restored.
She turns to a God who allows his people to suffer from
famine, but who comforts them and redeems them.[49]

The rabbis considered Ruth's speech to constitute her formal
declaration of becoming a proselyte to the Law (*Ruth Rabbah* 2.22),
though she remains known as a "Moabite" throughout the story. In light
of her strong allegiance to Yahweh, Ruth is often compared to Abraham
and his willingness to leave family and home for a land God would show
him (cf. Josh 24:2). In fact, "Ruth's action is even more memorable than
Abraham's for she acts without a specific revelation from God, without
any divine word of calling or blessing."[50]

Finally, Ruth's promise to be buried with Naomi in a new land was
incredibly significant, though it means little to us. Whereas "to most
Westerners, there is usually little emotional trauma in being buried away
from the family plot," it was absolutely understood in ancient times that
a person would be buried in their homeland[51] (cf. Gen 49:29–32; 50:25;
Amos 7:17). Ruth's faithfulness to Naomi would not be "until death," but
would rather transcend it. Her "commitment is total, not just in intensity
but also in duration."[52]

---

49. Nancy M. Tischler, "Ruth" in *A Complete Literary Guide to the Bible*, eds. Leland Ryken
and Tremper Longman III (Grand Rapids: Zondervan, 1993), 163.

50. Sakenfeld, *Ruth*, 33. "Divine promise motivated and sustained [Abraham's] leap of
faith. Besides, Abraham was a man, with a wife and other possessions to accompany him. Ruth
stands alone; she possesses nothing. No God has called her; no deity has promised her blessing;
no human being has come to her aid. She lives and chooses without a support group, and she
knows that the fruit of her decision may well be the emptiness of rejection, indeed of death.
Consequently, not even Abraham's leap of faith surpasses this decision of Ruth's," (Phyllis Trible,
God and the Rhetoric of Sexuality [Philadelphia: Fortress, 1978], 173).

51. Manor, "Ruth," 248.

52. Auld, *Ruth*, 263.

As far as she knew, Ruth was surrendering any legitimate hope of remarriage, children, and economic stability in her old age. But more significantly—and this is often missed by modern readers—Ruth was abandoning "all the primary markers of her identity as a Moabite."[53] If anything, moving to a new country and culture would prompt one to hold on tighter to expressions of ethnic and cultural identity, but none of that mattered to Ruth. She put Naomi's needs above her own, providing us with a wonderful illustration of Christ-glorifying love (1 Cor 13:4).[54]

Ruth even swore an oath (1:17) to follow Naomi to the grave and took upon herself the wrath of God if she did not keep her promise. It is likely that Ruth made a gesture with her hand across her throat in a slashing motion, symbolizing what she wanted God to do to her if she failed to keep her promise.[55] The NASU translates the Hebrew more literally: "Thus may the LORD do to me, and worse." This was a common method of making a vow in those days; the phrase she uttered is found, in varying forms, eleven other places in the OT.[56] Ziegler says, "Ruth's deliberate decision to employ the name of the LORD, rather than the general usage of the name of God, underscores her active and total acceptance of the personal God of Israel. At the same time, it is a deliberate and conscious rejection of any other god."[57]

---

53. Driesbach, "Ruth," 518.

54. "With radical self-sacrifice [Ruth] abandons every base of security that any person, let alone a poor widow, in that cultural context would have clung to: her native homeland, her own people, even her own gods," (Block, *Ruth*, 641).

55. "Deep behind this lay, in all probability, a ritual act involving the slaughter of animals, to whom the one swearing the oath equated himself. The best indications that this is so are the portrayals of elaborate covenant ratifications, containing solemn oaths, in Gen 15:7–17 and Jer 34:18–20. The slaughtered and split animals represent what the oath-taker invites God to do to him if he fails to keep the oath," (Edward F. Campbell, Jr., *Ruth* [Garden City, NY: Doubleday, 1975], 74).

56. 1 Sam 3:17; 14:44; 20:13; 25:22; 2 Sam 3:9, 35; 19:14; 1 Kgs 2:23; 19:2; 20:10; 2 Kgs 6:31. For more, see Manfred R. Lehman, "Biblical Oaths," *ZAW* 81 (1969): 74–92.

57. Yael Ziegler, "'So Shall God Do…': Variations of an Oath Formula and Its Literary Meaning," *JBL* 126 (2007): 59–81; cf. Hubbard, *Book of Ruth*, 120.

We don't know every reason why Ruth remained with Naomi, socially absurd as it was. Regardless of her reasons, God used Ruth's faithfulness to impact Naomi's life for the better. He can, and will, use you to do the same for someone else's life. We need only let him work through us.

RUTH 1:19–22

Naomi's return to Bethlehem created lots of excitement and commotion (cf. 1 Sam 4:5; 1 Kgs 1:45). The town's population was likely no more than a few hundred people, and even this number would have been diminished somewhat by the famine.[58] If you think about it, it is little wonder that Naomi's friends scarcely recognized her: "This one who had left Bethlehem as *Naomi*, 'the pleasant one,' a robust woman in her prime, had returned as a haggard and destitute old woman."[59] It had been at least a decade since Elimelech's family had left for greener pastures. We all know individuals whose physical appearance has been dramatically and heartbreakingly altered by the storms of life.

I'm particularly struck by Naomi's language—"I went away full, and the LORD has brought me back empty." Naomi thought of herself as complete when she and her family moved to Moab to escape the famine ravaging her homeland. How could she be "full" when her plate was empty? Naomi, of course, was referring to her family; she didn't feel empty when her husband and sons were by her side. All of us would agree that, when a person is a part of a family, unspeakable trials are more easily endured. If that family is stripped away, however, and we are forced to walk the Bethlehem Road alone, we feel empty and forsaken.

---

58. Lawrence E. Stager, "The Archaeology of the Family in Early Israel," *BASOR* 260 (1985): 1–35; cf. William G. Dever, "Israel, History of (Archaeology and the Israelite 'Conquest')," ABD 3:549; Manor, "Ruth," 248; Walton, *Bible Background*, 278.

59. Block, *Ruth*, 645. "Moffatt brings out something of the wordplay in the Hebrew with, *call me Mara, for the Almighty has cruelly marred me*," (Leon Morris, "Ruth" in *Judges & Ruth* [Downers Grove, IL: Inter-Varsity Press, 1968], 262).

Every line and wrinkle on Naomi's face would have betrayed the bitterness and pain of her soul. She had escaped the famine and was "physically alive, but from an emotional and psychological point of view, she views her life as already over."[60] In Scripture, bitterness and loss go hand-in-hand, whether it is the loss of property (1 Sam 22:2) or loved ones (Ezek 27:30–31; Amos 8:10), particularly children (1 Sam 1:10; 30:6; 2 Kgs 4:27; Zech 12:10). Naomi explained that God was the source of her calamity and loss (cf. 1 Kgs 17:20; Job 27:2). Notice that the narrator does not agree or disagree with her statement, but simply repeats what she said without further comment. Thus, the audience is left to wonder: Was God the true source of her sadness?

Naomi's choice of monikers for God—"the Almighty" (1:20)—is particularly noteworthy. The Hebrew *shaddai* was a title for Yahweh and "is associated with his cosmic power, his authority to judge, to bless or to curse."[61] The title is rather uncommon in the OT, occurring only 48 times, whereas Yahweh appears 6,800 times.[62] What is interesting is that 31 of *shaddai's* 48 occurrences are in Job. God as the Almighty must be an important concept to those who are suffering, whether used as a source of comfort—"God is in control, so his light will soon dispel this darkness" (cf. Rom 8:28)—or cause of bitterness—"God is in control, so why has he made me suffer like this?" (cf. Judg 6:13). "When the world is crashing in, we need assurance that God reigns over it all."[63]

The chapter ends with a note explaining that Naomi and Ruth's arrival had come "at the beginning of barley harvest." This detail provides

---

60. Sakenfeld, *Ruth*, 36.

61. Driesbach, "Ruth," 519.

62. "Since Naomi regularly uses God's more common name, yhwh, her choice here must convey something specific," (Eskenazi, *Ruth*, 24).

63. Piper, *Sweet and Bitter Providence*, 27. He later adds, "I would take Naomi's theology any day over the sentimental views of God that permeate so many churches today. Endless excuses are made for God's sovereignty. Naomi is unshaken and sure about three things: God exists, God is sovereign, and God has afflicted her," (Ibid., 37–38).

a natural segue to the next scene. In ancient Israel, barley was normally harvested in mid- or late-April, and wheat about a month later. But the statement is meant to represent more than a scene change or date stamp—it is a clue to what lies ahead. Naomi's life was a desolate famine of disappointment, but God was about to bring a rich harvest of blessings. He was already at work, redeeming her bitterness for his own glory and her good.[64] He would soon make her whole once more.

When my wife rocks our son to sleep, she often sings softly to him, "My God is so big, so strong, and so mighty; there's nothing my God cannot do." Growing up, my parents imparted that same conviction to me: God is all-powerful, and nothing is impossible for him. So you can understand why my dad's untimely death threatened to undermine my relationship with the Lord. If God were both all-loving and all-powerful, he could have easily prevented my dad's death. It would not have been complicated—just cause the wind to blow in a different direction, or not at all. Like Naomi, I felt as if the Lord's hand had gone out against me when my dad died—that God was seeking to make my life bitter.

There are times when it seems so obvious that God must be against us. At those times, however, it may be that we are overlooking subtle signs that God remains firmly in our corner (Rom 8:31–39). Naomi felt empty, bereft, lost—but she still had Ruth! Naomi felt God was against her—but he had visited his people with food so that Naomi could return home to her family in Bethlehem!

Sometimes blaming God for our problems only blinds us to his providence. We become so overwhelmed by what we have suffered or lost that we can no longer see him before us. "What would Naomi say if she

---

64. "The portrait's dark colors prepare the reader theologically for the story's conclusion. Since only Yahweh can do the impossible, one will recognize Yahweh's intervention when the unreal becomes reality," (Hubbard, *Book of Ruth*, 111).

could see only a fraction of the thousands of things God was doing in the bitter providences of her life?"[65]

A decade later, despite the grief and pain, I still believe that "My God is so big, so strong, and so mighty; there's nothing my God cannot do." I've also learned, however, that it's foolish to try and figure out God through the lens of life's circumstances. Instead, we should interpret life's circumstances through the lens of what we know about God and his character as revealed in Scripture.[66]

I've also learned not to try and salvage God's reputation at the expense of his sovereignty. Some Christians try to explain why bad things happen to good people in a way that actually undermines the great biblical truth of God always being in control. They would rather live in a universe where some things are just bad luck if it means defending God as a deity who never hurts our feelings or acts against our will. When God finally broke his silence to Job, after all that the patriarch had endured, the Lord's message was a clear affirmation that he was still on top of things (Job 38–41).

While walking the Bethlehem Road, I would rather serve an Almighty God who acts mysteriously at times, but is in complete control (cf. Job 13:15), rather than a God who never hurts my feelings because he is pathetically impotent or apathetic to his children. I would also prefer to believe that God is always at work for his glory and my good, instead of believing that he only works sometimes, letting bad things happen when he is "on a break," or that bad things slip by him like a soccer ball past the goalie.[67] We are not told of God's direct involvement in Naomi's plight, whether he struck down her husband and sons because of sin, or whether he allowed Satan to take their lives as part of a grander plan (cf. Job 1:6–19). There is one thing, however, we can know for certain that is as true

---

65. Piper, *Sweet and Bitter Providence*, 42.

66. Hamilton, *Handbook*, 192–93.

67. "God does not act intermittently, but continuously. Though He may appear to step into the scene at given key moments, He is actually and actively there *every* moment, albeit hidden," (Jackman, *Ruth*, 319).

now as it was in Naomi's day: God does not allow anything to happen that he cannot redeem for his glory and our good.

TALKING POINTS

The final verse of the book of Judges reminds us of our own subjective world, and how broken relationships are often a casualty of our sin. Few individuals practice unconditional faithfulness and true devotion anymore. Too many times, we use people for as long as they are necessary, only to discard them when they become expendable. We do what is right in our own eyes, but the rotting corpses of our broken relationships are monuments to our moral failure and rebellious sin. The story of Ruth reminds us that relationships are not cheap bonds to be broken when circumstances require—or our selfishness demands it. Rather, loyalty in any relationship is a sacred obligation.[68] In marriage, a couple vows before God to be loyal to one another until death. As Christians, we rejoice in Christ's promise to be faithful to us beyond the grave (Matt 28:20; 2 Tim 2:13). But Jesus also expects us to be devoted to one another just as he is devoted to us. This is an important message for church members who expect the church to minister to them in their self-absorption, instead of searching out opportunities to minister to others. "If the Galatians 6:2 instruction to 'carry each other's burdens' has any meaning, certainly Ruth's actions are an evidence of it. Where we can help ease the pain of individuals within the body of believers, we should do *hesed*."[69]

Ruth's faithfulness to her mother-in-law became the only flickering candle of hope in Naomi's otherwise shattered world. Had it not been for such faithfulness, Naomi would have never seen God's faithfulness in her life.[70] The emotional scars of abandonment, betrayal,

---

68. "Loyalty ties individuals together. True loyalty is seldom easy. It takes both patience and a willingness to be inconvenienced. Genuinely loyal people adjust their schedules to meet the needs of those they serve. Loyalty often comes at a price." (*The Charles F. Stanley Life Principles Bible* [Nashville: Nelson, 2005], 309).

69. Younger, *Ruth*, 436.

70. "Although *hesed* in Ruth is explicitly ascribed to human beings, the text suggests that those who act with *hesed* mirror the ways of God, serving as agents of God's *hesed* through their

and loneliness can be devastating. There are those who recover and go on
to live productive lives, but others never recover at all. Our faithfulness
could be the final thread of hope to which the lost and despairing cling
in their darkest hour. Showing such individuals the faithful love of Christ
could pay eternal dividends![71] Our *unfaithfulness*, on the other hand, has
the power to shatter someone's life. My dad bore the emotional scars of
having been abandoned by his parents at age six, not to mention being
betrayed in his early twenties by an adulterous adopted father. Despite the
darkness in his past, my dad was able to rise above his suffering, but only
because of the faithful love and constant support of my mom. He often
told me that a person must choose to be bitter or better. He rose above his
suffering, but others never do. Our unfaithfulness can shatter lives.

T he role of community in the grief-recovery process cannot be
underestimated. It was providential that God "visited" Israel with
food just when Naomi's life had seemingly fallen apart. Yahweh wanted
Naomi to return to her clan in Bethlehem, to the house of Israel, so that
she would be better comforted in her pain. We likewise can imagine that
he sent Ruth to comfort her along the way. Those who walk the Bethlehem
Road should seek comfort amidst God's people, the church. Just as the
human body supports a part of itself that is suffering and in pain, so too
must the church support its members when they suffer (1 Cor 12:26). In
the covenant community, the faithfulness and providential care of God
is revealed through the faithful concern, generosity, and goodness of his
people. It is also in the church that we learn to trust God again. When in
the throes of grief, it is very tempting to withdraw into a self-imposed

---

deeds of kindness," (Eskenazi, *Ruth*, 1).

71. "What changed Ruth's life? It wasn't a sermon. It wasn't programs. It wasn't a great
book. It wasn't incredible arguments. ... It all happened through nothing but a friendship, and
there's nothing else to it. Friendship is about the only way I know to change somebody's life,"
(Timothy J. Keller, "An Immigrant's Courage" in *The Timothy Keller Sermon Archive* [New York:
Redeemer Presbyterian Church, 2013]).

prison of isolated despair. We must allow God to draw us out of ourselves and into the arms of friends and fellow Christians; only then will we know joy and peace on the Bethlehem Road.

Admittedly, there is tension in this story that is difficult to explain. Naomi prayed that God would show kindness to her daughters-in-law, but when her focus turned inward, she could only rant of how God had deserted her. Her attitudes in 1:8–9 and 1:13, 20 are very different. There is no doubt that Naomi "ascribe[d] sovereignty to God, but this is a sovereignty without grace, an omnipotent power without compassion, a judicial will without mercy."[72] Naomi was unimaginably bitter and blamed God for her suffering, a common stage in the grief process. In the story, Ruth's faithful love stands opposite of Naomi's bitterness.[73] Especially in the early stages of grief, the last thing the bereaved should hear from us is spiritual correction (e.g. "You shouldn't feel that way/say things like that") or phony attempts at empathy ("I know how you feel; my _____ died recently"). Nor do they need theological explanations for their suffering; the funeral home is the worst place to correct someone's theology. However, I understand the compulsion to say *something*. In that light, "I'm sorry" and "I love you" can do a world of good—anything else in the house of mourning is likely inappropriate. All you need to do is let that person know you are there for them; they will remember your offer of support and seek you out when they are ready.

A particularly sad detail about Naomi's return to Bethlehem was that she never truly acknowledged Ruth. Instead, she focused on her own bitterness and sorrow, believing God was punishing her. Naomi was so blinded by her grief and pain that she couldn't see Ruth's presence for the blessing it was. "Like many of Job's speeches, Naomi's anguished, reactive

---

72. Block, *Ruth*, 647.

73. Younger, *Ruth*, 432.

speech to the women of Bethlehem demonstrates one of the unfortunate truths of suffering: In the midst of pain, there is often self-absorption. ... Such self-absorption in the midst of pain and affliction is understandable. Yet it always blinds a person from God's greater plan and the small ways in which God may be working this plan out."[74] Whenever we are at our lowest points, it's easy to buy into the lie that God has abandoned us and left us with no help or recourse for our troubles. Self-pity is Satan's way of blinding us to the glory and hope of providence. If we are willing to look beyond ourselves, however, we will discover that God's blessings in the bad times are still more numerous and more powerful than anything Satan can contrive. Naomi had a faithful daughter-in-law who proved to be better than seven sons (4:15). She also had a community of friends and relatives, a kinsman-redeemer named Boaz, and the mysterious, providential hand of Yahweh. Naomi was anything but empty.

---

74. Ibid., 432–33.

2

THE MYSTERIOUS HAND

Providence is an odd thing. What Jesus said about the wind could easily be applied to providence's mysterious hand: "You hear its sound, but you do not know where it comes from or where it goes" (John 3:8).

In early 1985, a medical student "just happened" to start working weekends in the ER of a small Mississippi town. Being a faithful Christian, he attended worship at the church across from the hospital, and there met my parents. "Why don't you spend the night in our guest room whenever you're in town?" they asked Tim. He eagerly accepted the offer. Thirty years later, Tim held my son in his arms and played with him, just like my dad would have done were he still alive. My son, Daniel, will never know his grandpa and namesake in this life, but knowing men like Tim is the next best thing. Even now, I'm misty-eyed as I think about how Tim and Pam have been faithful to three generations of Whitworths. What began as a simple expression of hospitality from my parents has blossomed into a family friendship that has taught me the meaning of *hesed* and has blessed my life in countless ways.

This is providence.

In October 2004, a month after my dad had suddenly passed away, a peppy blonde freshman girl "just happened" to walk up to me and say, "Hi, I'm Amanda. Our dads went to college together, and I want you to know I've been praying for you." She soon began dating a friend of mine, who gave his blessing to my platonic relationship with his girlfriend; he knew I desperately needed every friend I could get during that bitter season of my life. A year later, Amanda introduced me to her dad, who was visiting campus at the time. Since that day, September 19, 2005, Jeff and his wife, Laura, have treated me better than I ever deserve. They think of my wife as a daughter and of my son as their grandchild. What began as a simple expression of care and concern from a young woman has blossomed into multiple deep friendships that have blessed my life in countless ways.

This is providence.

In February 2009, I "just happened" to get on Facebook late one Saturday night while watching college basketball. I "just happened" to start chatting with a girl I had known as a teenager. Eight weeks later, Sara and I eloped. She has been, and remains, an amazing God-send to my life. My only regret is that I didn't ask her to marry me sooner. I love and am grateful for her more than my words can adequately express. What began with a simple "Hey" has blossomed into a marriage that has blessed my life in countless ways.

This is providence.

Providence is an odd thing. To the uninitiated, it goes by the blasphemous titles of fate, luck, chance, karma, or happenstance. The people of God, however, know that providence is the mysterious hand of "the One who makes everything agree with what he decides and wants" (Eph 1:11 NCV).

The mystery of providence, however, is how dependent it is on human action. For example, what if my parents had never offered Tim their guest room? What if he had chosen some other ER in some other town while he wrapped up medical school? What if Amanda simply had *intentions* of offering me her condolences, but never followed through in expressing them? What if her then-boyfriend/now-husband hadn't considered our relationship to be kosher? What if Jeff had met me, but never had the heart (and courage) to befriend a fatherless young minister? What if I had started chatting with some other person on Facebook that

Saturday night? What if I had been more interested in the matchup on ESPN between Texas and #2 Oklahoma?

I don't have answers for all the mysterious questions of providence, but I know that God takes our actions, large and small, and works them into his plan. Wiersbe is right: "God is constantly working *with us* (Mark 16:20), *in us* (Phil. 2:12–13), and *for us* (Rom. 8:28) and accomplishing His gracious purposes. We pray, we seek His will, and we make decisions (and sometimes make mistakes); but it is God who orders events and guides His willing children."[1]

It is often the case that our stubbornness and pain blinds us to God's activity in our lives. Our bitterness can mask divine providence, convincing us that God has forgotten us—or worse, as Naomi believed, that he is out to get us. But the eyes of faith see God at work in the past and present for our good and redemption and deliverance. In a similar way, the eyes of faith believe that God will go before us on the Bethlehem Road to bring us peace and joy again. As we still believe in the sun on a cloudy day, so we must continue to trust in God's presence and power when life's storms obscure him from view.

The previous chapter taught us the importance of being faithful in all our relationships, just as Ruth was faithful to Naomi. In this chapter, Ruth and Boaz will impress on us the truth that God uses the obedience of his people to comfort the brokenhearted and redeem their suffering. He orchestrates our past and present faithfulness for our future blessing.

RUTH 2:1–7

The barley harvest had commenced, and we are introduced to Naomi's distant relative by marriage. His name was Boaz, a "worthy" (ESV) or "prominent" (HCSB) man (cf. "a man of standing," NIV). Elsewhere in the OT, the Hebrew phrase has obvious militaristic connotations (cf. Judg 6:12) and is translated "mighty man of valor" (Josh 6:2; 2 Sam 17:8; 2 Kgs

---

1. Warren W. Wiersbe, *Be Committed* (Wheaton, IL: Victor, 1993), 29.

24:16). It can also refer to one possessing talent (1 Kgs 11:28; Neh 11:14) or great wealth (2 Kgs 15:20); Morris suggests that the English concept of a knight is quite similar.[2] Boaz, then, was a wealthy and well-respected pillar of the Bethlehem community,[3] one who had perhaps distinguished himself in battle during the many military excursions common of the Judges period. He was no "ordinary, run-of-the-mill Israelite,"[4] and as we are about to discover, he would further distinguish himself as a friend of the poor, meaning he was also wise (cf. Prov 14:31; 22:9).

Boaz, we learn, owned a field in which Ruth sought to glean and gather grain. In ancient Israel, reaping grain consisted of workers (likely paid, not slaves) grabbing large handfuls of stalks and cutting them with a sickle (Deut 16:9; Jer 50:16), which would have had a flint blade in Ruth's time.[5] These handfuls were collected, bound together into sheaves, and transported to the threshing floor.

Under the Law of Moses, landowners were not permitted "to harvest the full extent of their fields, but they were to leave produce in the hard-to-reach areas. The remaining harvest was for the poor and foreigners who might be in the land,"[6] (Lev 19:9–10; 23:22; Deut 24:19–22). This practice continued among Arabs in the Middle East until recent times.[7] The bugaboo, however, was that Ruth's story occurred in the days of the Judges when the majority of Israel adhered to the Law with as much gusto

---

2.   "We perhaps get the force of it by thinking of our word 'knight'. This applied originally to a man distinguished for military prowess, but it is now used widely of those whose excellence lies in other fields," (Morris, "Ruth," 269).

3.   In what is either a terrific coincidence or linguistic connection, the north pillar of Solomon's Temple was also called "Boaz" (1 Kgs 7:21; 2 Chr 3:17).

4.   Jack M. Sasson, *Ruth*, 2nd ed. (Sheffield: Sheffield Academic, 1989), 40.

5.   Oded Borowski, "Harvests, Harvesting," ABD 3:64.

6.   Manor, "Ruth," 251. He goes on to mention a similar "law" in Egypt: "'[Do not] pounce on a widow when you find her in the fields. And then fail to be patient with her reply.' It is not clear if this instruction reflects a widespread custom or law in Egypt or if it simply represents Amenemope's perception of civility and humanitarianism," (Ibid., 252).

7.   Gray, *Ruth*, 390.

as American motorists obey speed limits. "Greedy owners and reapers probably often obstructed the efforts of gleaners by ridicule, tricks, and in some cases outright expulsion."[8] In other words, there was no guarantee that any landowner in Bethlehem's vicinity would intentionally leave leftovers for the poor, let alone a poor Gentile widow.

Knowing that the barley harvest was happening, Ruth sought Naomi's permission to glean in the fields.[9] The narrator says she "happened to come to the part of the field belonging to Boaz," as if Ruth unknowingly lucked out on this decision, but "the chance encounter turns out to be a sovereign setup of circumstances."[10] The narrator's many references to chance, luck, fate, or happenstance are always made tongue-in-cheek:[11] "The lot is cast into the lap, but its every decision is from the LORD" (Prov 16:33). It is clear that Yahweh—the God whom Naomi thought was out to get her— was working events for the good of Naomi, Ruth, and Boaz, as well as for the sake of his own great name. That Ruth chose the field of a worthy man like Boaz—who followed the Law when so many others did not—wasn't luck at all, but providence from the Giver of every good gift (Jas 1:17).

On that particular day, when Boaz arrived to supervise his workers and monitor the day's activities, he noticed Ruth among the other women trailing the reapers. There is more here than meets the eye. Boaz asked

---

8.   Hubbard, *Book of Ruth*, 136.

9.   It's possible that Ruth opted to glean in Naomi's stead "because she wanted to shield the once wealthy Naomi from the shame of their reduced circumstances," (Eskenazi, *Ruth*, 28). It would have been like seeing Vanderbilts or Rockefellers in line at the Salvation Army soup kitchen. "Granting permission to Ruth to glean alongside the rest of the institutionalized poor is the point where Naomi hits rock bottom," (Moore, "Ruth," 328).

10.   D. L. Petter, "Ruth" in *The Baker Illustrated Bible Commentary* (Grand Rapids: Baker, 2012), 249.

11.   "By excessively attributing Ruth's good fortune to chance, he forces the reader to sit up and take notice, to ask questions concerning the significance of everything that is transpiring. The statement is ironical; its purpose is to undermine purely rational explanations for human experiences and to refine the reader's understanding of providence. In reality he is screaming, 'See the hand of God at work here!'" (Block, *Ruth*, 653). Eskenazi isn't so sure that providence is at play here (*Ruth*, 27).

about this new woman, and his overseer reported that Ruth had asked to glean in the field. The ESV translates the overseer's words as, "She came, and she has continued from early morning until now, except for a short rest." But in the original language, this verse is an unmitigated mess. The Hebrew text of 2:7 either has been corrupted or was intentionally left ambiguous by the author for narrative effect,[12] leaving the impression that Ruth was either molested or the subject of racial prejudice. Younger persuasively recreates the context:

> As he [the overseer] is speaking [to Boaz], Ruth is at some distance from them, with her back turned to Boaz, and she is on her way out of the field because of an incident of what today we would call sexual harassment, which she experienced when she sought a drink of water. Thus, the translation of the last words of verse 7 might be something like: "This fellow … ah, she's just going home for a bit." The foreman starts his explanation, becomes embarrassed, and tries to make some lame excuse.[13]

Obviously, it's impossible to know for sure if Ruth had been molested, or if these were merely precautions. But if nothing had happened, it only means something hadn't happened *yet*.[14] A young immigrant widow, presumably an attractive one, being without a male protector (e.g. father, brother, husband), and working among common laborers was not a safe situation. Moreover, the overseer's report depicts him as very unwilling

---

12. Younger renders the Hebrew of 2:7 as literally reading, "this (masc.) her sitting the house (a) little," (*Ruth*, 443). Campbell (*Ruth*, 94) concedes, "It is likely that the precise meaning here will permanently elude us." For more on the difficulty of 2:7, see Daniel Lys, "Résidence ou repos? Notule sur Ruth ii 7," *VT* 21 (1971): 497–501; Michael S. Moore, "Two Textual Anomalies in Ruth," *CBQ* 59 (1997): 234–43.

13. Younger, *Ruth*, 444; cf. Michael Carasik, "Ruth 2,7: Why the Overseer Was Embarrassed," *ZAW* 107 (1995): 493–94.

14. David Shepherd, "Violence in the Fields" Translating, Reading, and Revising in Ruth 2," *CBQ* 63 (2001): 459.

to let Ruth glean in the fields,[15] and that he hoped the boss would agree. Ruth later thanked Boaz for calming her nerves and putting her mind at ease (2:13), so it seems her arrival at the field had not been particularly welcome by Boaz's men.

RUTH 2:8–16

Having learned about her from his overseer, Boaz approached Ruth and gave assurances concerning her being welcome and protected on his land.[16] Being a widowed immigrant, and working in the fields (cf. Deut 22:25–27), Ruth would have been a tempting target for abuse and mistreatment in any society, how much more so in Israel during the Judges period? In fact, Boaz's use of "touch" in 2:9 could possibly refer to rape (cf. Gen 20:6; Prov 6:29), but more likely notes any sort of physical or verbal abuse (cf. Gen 26:11, 29; Josh 8:15).

Boaz also encouraged Ruth not to be shy about drinking water from the same vessels as his workers. These would have been clay pots or goatskin bags[17] filled with water drawn from the well near Bethlehem's gate (2 Sam 23:16; 1 Chr 11:18), and being allowed to drink from these vessels (rather than fetching her own water) would have saved Ruth considerable time. Moreover, "in a cultural context in which normally foreigners would draw for Israelites, and women would draw for men (Gen 24:10–20), Boaz's authorization of Ruth to drink from water his men had drawn is indeed extraordinary."[18]

To this warm welcome and promise of protection, Ruth bowed and inquired why Boaz was being so gracious, especially when she was

---

15. Jonathan Grossman, "'Gleaning among the Ears'—'Gathering among the Sheaves': Characterizing the Image of the Supervising Boy (Ruth 2)," *JBL* 126 (2007): 703–16.

16. "From the outset Boaz makes it clear to this widow that her wandering days are over," (Moore, "Ruth," 332). Coffman lists no fewer than ten acts of kindness by Boaz towards Ruth in this scene (James Burton Coffman, *Judges and Ruth* [Abilene, TX: ACU Press, 1992], 349–50).

17. Hubbard, *Book of Ruth*, 160.

18. Block, *Ruth*, 660.

an immigrant.[19] In her actions and words, "the symbolism was graphic: her vulnerable prostration physically expressed both the social distance between them and her gratitude for Boaz's kindness."[20] His reply was this:

> All that you have done for your mother-in-law since the death of your husband has been fully told to me, and how you left your father and mother and your native land and came to a people that you did not know before. The LORD repay you for what you have done, and a full reward be given you by the LORD, the God of Israel, under whose wings you have come to take refuge!
>
> Ruth 2:11–12

In short, Ruth's faithfulness—shown in her following Naomi to Bethlehem, and thereby eschewing the security and refuge of her parents' house for a very uncertain future in a foreign land as an immigrant widow—spoke volumes about Ruth's character. It is, after all, "loyalty [that] makes a person attractive" (Prov 19:22 NLT). Boaz knew this and invoked Yahweh's blessing on her, petitioning the Lord to repay her extraordinary act of *hesed*. The verb Boaz used has a variety of meanings, including "to complete," "to make whole," or "to restore."[21] In this light, Boaz was not inferring that God owed Ruth a debt, but that Yahweh was the only one who could restore the safety and security she had forsaken when she decided to follow Naomi to a foreign land.

Boaz also acknowledged that Ruth had converted to Israel's religion by seeking refuge under the wings of the God of Israel. The imagery is a

---

19. The Hebrew word rendered "foreigner" was often used of non-Israelites in a pejorative or deprecating way (cf. Exod 21:8; Deut 17:15; Job 19:15; Ezra 10:10; Neh 13:26). Coffman makes an excellent point when he observes, "Boaz himself was a descendant of Rahab the Gentile of Jericho, and it might have been that he was more readily disposed to accept such a foreigner as Ruth than other Israelites might have been," (*Ruth*, 349).

20. Hubbard, *Book of Ruth*, 161.

21. Moore, "Ruth," 335.

wonderful one; as a hen protects her chicks or an eagle shelters her young from predators and storms, so God spreads his wings over his people. Particularly in the OT, "wings of refuge" was "a commonly used figure of speech for God's over-arching and protective presence"[22] (Deut 32:11–12; Pss 17:8; 36:7; 57:1; 61:4; 63:7; 91:1, 4), imagery echoed by Christ in the NT (Matt 23:37; Luke 13:34). In artwork from the ANE, "deities with wings are often portrayed overshadowing the king."[23] The God of Israel cares for more than the rich, the powerful, or the popular; he also cares for lowly immigrant widows. Here, Ruth is depicted as a young bird escaping the storms of life by seeking shelter under the providential wings of Yahweh.[24] She wasn't a random immigrant seeking a handout; she had forsaken her pagan background and staked her personal future on the *hesed* of Israel's God.

Ruth's response to Boaz is noteworthy. She was especially grateful that Boaz had given her comfort, meaning relieved tensions or an easing of the mind.[25] It is difficult to put ourselves in Ruth's shoes and realize how unlikely it was that a man in Boaz's position would take notice of such a woman. She acknowledged that she had found "favor" in Boaz's eyes (cf. "Why have you been so kind to notice me?" NCV) and humbled herself before him. In classifying herself as a "servant" (2:13), Ruth placed herself at the bottom of the social hierarchy of her day (a place still occupied by many widows today, immigrant and native). Moreover, she specified that, while she was a servant, she was not a servant of Boaz, thereby removing

---

22. Wesley J. Fuerst, *The Books of Ruth, Esther, Ecclesiastes, the Song of Songs, Lamentations* (Cambridge: Cambridge Univ. Press, 1975), 19.

23. Walton, *Bible Background*, 279.

24. "'There is no place like this: let us joyously abide together under the wing of God.' There is no rest, no peace, no calm, no perfect quiet, like that of giving up all care, because you cast your care on God; renouncing all fear, because your only fear is a fear of offending God. Oh the bliss of knowing that sooner may the universe be dissolved than the great heart that beats above you cease to be full of tenderness and love to all those that shelter beneath it," (C. H. Spurgeon, *The Metropolitan Tabernacle Pulpit Sermons*, vol. 31 [London: Passmore, 1885], 402–3).

25. Block, *Ruth*, 665.

herself entirely out of his circle. Thus, "Ruth is totally amazed that differences of race or class could not stifle Boaz's compassion toward her."[26]

In an extraordinary gesture of generosity, Boaz also welcomed Ruth to join him and his men at the luncheon table of fellowship. Boaz himself even served her some roasted grain[27] and invited her to dip her bread into the wine.[28] Ruth was also expected to eat until she was full, which she did.[29] In every sense, Boaz was a man with a big heart for the disenfranchised and ostracized of society.

The most magnanimous of Boaz's acts, however, was reserved for the end. While the Law mandated that landowners not reap their entire fields, Boaz went a step further, commanding his workers to allow Ruth to glean from the sheaves of grain already harvested, and even to encourage her in this by pulling out stalks of grain from the sheaves, a concession that meant Ruth had to expend less effort in her endeavor. Younger calls this "an unheard-of favor,"[30] particularly since the Mishnah (reflecting Jewish custom) strictly allowed gleaners to pick up *only* what had had been left behind by chance, and not what had been dropped because a worker's hand had been pricked by thorns (*Peah* 4.10)!

St. John of the Cross once said, "Look upon it as a special mercy of God that people ever speak kindly to you; you do not deserve it." Surviving the Bethlehem Road requires its travelers to unload the heavy

---

26. Block, *Ruth*, 665–66.

27. Roasted grain was a common staple in OT times (cf 1 Sam 17:17; 25:18; 2 Sam 17:28). They were most often "parched in a pan over the fire, or in some similar way, before they were eaten, (L. Berkhof, *Biblical Archaeology* [Grand Rapids: Eerdmans, 1915], 53).

28. This wine is "best understood as a sour sauce or condiment used to moisten and spice up dry bread. Boaz could not allow her to eat dry bread while he enjoyed more pleasant food," (Block, *Ruth*, 667).

29. "Since gleaners were so poor, a satisfactory meal was no small blessing," (Hubbard, *Book of Ruth*, 175). "Elsewhere in the Bible, being able to eat until satisfied is often the result of God's generosity (e.g., Deut. 6:11; 8:10; 11:15; 31:20). Thus, Boaz is already cast in the role of an agent bringing to fruition some of the blessings he wished for Ruth in 2:12," (Eskenazi, *Ruth*, 41).

30. Younger, *Ruth*, 446.

burden of privilege and entitlement[31] and instead consider "what we are owed" to be gracious, freely-given blessings from above. The Law might have entitled Ruth to glean in the fields, but she recognized Boaz's magnanimous generosity for what it was. Humble gratitude, instead of harsh entitlement, brings healing to a broken heart.

From one perspective, you and I don't deserve all the pain and sorrow life sends our way. But from another perspective, the heavenly one, we have no right to live another moment, nor enjoy any goodness at all. Our sins merit us a lifetime of misery and an eternity of suffering. But instead of giving us what we deserve, God caused Jesus to suffer in our place. Every blessing, every good thing, is a gift. Entitlement will make our days on the Bethlehem Road miserable, but gratitude will make every mile manageable and all the more triumphant.[32]

RUTH 2:17-23

Due to Boaz's enormous generosity, Ruth successfully gleaned "about an ephah of barley," the same amount of grain that her great-grandson David delivered to his three brothers on the front lines (1 Sam 17:17). Scholars are uncertain as to the exact amount of an ephah. Originally an Egyptian loanword that meant "basket" (and thus "basketful"),[33] one source states that an ephah was equal to two-thirds of a bushel, "which would have represented about a month's worth of the grain ration usually allotted to male workers."[34] In more practical terms, Hamlin says an ephah

---

31. "For [Ruth], sincere concern for her poverty was no reason to trample the rights of her neighbors. Instead, she sought to work within their prerogatives. That, also, is an admirable quality of devotion to be followed," (Hubbard, *Book of Ruth*, 150).

32. "Ruth neither looked back at her tragic past nor did she look at herself and consider her sorry plight. She fell at the feet of the master and submitted herself to him. She looked away from her poverty and focused on his riches. She forgot her fears and rested on his promises. What an example for God's people today to follow!" (Wiersbe, *Be Committed*, 32).

33. Hubbard, *Book of Ruth*, 179.

34. Walton, *Bible Background*, 279.

could feed two people for five to seven days,[35] while Goldingay compares an ephah to one's baggage allowance on a plane.[36] No matter the exact amount, it's clear that "to thresh an ephah of grain from one day's labor is an extraordinary feat, not to mention Ruth's having to carry it home! … The harvesters obviously followed Boaz's instructions and allowed Ruth to scavenge liberally."[37] What is more, if Ruth took home this same amount every day for the rest of the harvest (about seven weeks), she would have gleaned enough to feed her and Naomi for nearly a year!

When Ruth returned home with the day's produce, as well as a doggie bag from lunch, Naomi was understandably taken aback by the largesse. She asked her daughter-in-law, "Where did you glean today? And where have you worked? Blessed be the man who took notice of you" (2:19). When Naomi learned the identity of Ruth's gracious benefactor, it was as if "the sun rises again in her life. Yahweh has been gracious to her deceased husband and her sons by sending a potential 'redeemer-kinsman' into their lives."[38] She knew this was not fate or happenstance, but divine providence. Perhaps Yahweh's hand was no longer against her.

> Naomi knows something about [Boaz] that Ruth does not, and of which we ourselves have seen only a glimmer before this. Boaz is not just a relative, but a "close" relative, or "kinsman-redeemer" (a gō'ēl, 2:20). It is one of those crystallizing moments in a story when the plot changes gear, and latent possibilities suddenly rise to the surface. For Naomi is aware of the special obligations that devolve on a gō'ēl in Israelite law and custom. She is energized by hope, and suddenly able to see, not only her circumstances,

---

35. E. John Hamlin, *Surely There Is a Future* (Grand Rapids: Eerdmans, 1996), 35.

36. Goldingay, *Ruth*, 175.

37. Block, *Ruth*, 670.

38. Ibid., 676.

> but God himself, in a new light. ... In the kindness of Boaz
> Naomi perceives the kindness of Yahweh.[39]

Naomi encouraged Ruth not to deviate from gleaning in Boaz's fields, but to remain among the other women. It was in Ruth's best interests to do so, since she would always enjoy protection as one who had found favor in Boaz's eyes. Naomi, however, was also sensitive to the fact that, should Ruth glean in another field for whatever reason, Boaz might interpret it as a rejection of his magnanimous generosity.[40] In addition, remaining in his field meant "Ruth and Boaz would see each other again, perhaps even regularly. Who knows what might happen next, especially if, as the audience assumed, Yahweh lurked about?"[41]

The chapter ends with a note that Ruth continued to live with Naomi and glean in Boaz's fields for the next six to seven weeks, or until the end of the barley and wheat harvests—which would have been early June. The reader is left wondering what would become of these two widows. Boaz's largesse has been enormous this harvest season, but such will not feed Naomi and Ruth forever. Something else had to happen to redeem them from permanent poverty.

When Naomi returned to Bethlehem, she considered her life to be a bitter existence, and that God was out to get her. But God's hand had gone out for her good, not against her for her detriment. Naomi had simply become too bitter to see his presence and eternal love. God is faithful to his people, and he wields his mysterious hand of providence in

---

39. Webb, *Five Festal Garments*, 45.

40. Robert A. Jamieson, A. R. Fausset, and David Brown, *A Commentary Critical, Experimental and Practical on the Old and New Testament*, vol. 3 (Grand Rapids: Eerdmans, 1948), 131. "Has the Lord dealt bountifully with us? Let us not be found in any other field," (Matthew Henry, *Commentary on the Whole Bible*, vol. 2 [New York: Revell, 1935], 266).

41. Hubbard, *Book of Ruth*, 191.

order to provide for our needs. Long ago, God gave the Law to provide for widows in Naomi's position. He raised up a worthy man, Boaz, who would show generosity to Ruth. God is always at work in mysterious ways, though his purposes sometimes remain hidden from us.

Are you struggling on the Bethlehem Road? Is your burden of grief or pain too heavy? Do you feel as if God must be out to get you since you are being made to endure such terrible circumstances? Consider for a moment that it only *seems* that way because you don't have the advantage of knowing the future. Naomi could not know that God was working for her good, but that's where faith plays such a powerful part in dealing with suffering. Faith in God's power, love, and providence is necessary if we are to survive the Bethlehem Road. I have often heard faith derided by some as a crutch for weak people. But a crutch is quite helpful when you're walking lame on the Bethlehem Road.

TALKING POINTS

As a mighty man of Bethlehem, Boaz is a powerful example of someone willing to show *hesed* to more than just his family, clan, or close circle of friends. Here, we see him also extending extraordinary generosity to an immigrant widow, one far beneath his social station. Like Boaz, our *hesed* must not be a respecter of persons. Nor must our *hesed* be a respecter of places. If this particular episode had taken place in a religious context, one would expect kindness to be shown to Ruth. Boaz's *hesed*, however, was exhibited in the daily workplace, the place where we often fail miserably to show *hesed* to those who need it.[42] Webb reminds us that, "to put on kindness is to clothe ourselves with the very character of God himself."[43] The NT is replete with examples of how we are to love and forgive based on how God has loved and forgiven us (1 John 4:19; Eph 4:32). How might our relationships be richer if we were better reflectors of the faithful love of Christ? Who outside of our circles, or below our social station, is in need of our kindness?

There is something to be said for how Boaz went about expressing such incredible generosity to this young immigrant widow. He never drew attention to himself, and when Ruth pressed for an explanation as to Boaz's kindness, his reply was about what *she* had done, rather than centered on himself. Indeed, not until Naomi explained to Ruth just how Boaz was related to the family did Ruth fully understand the day's events: "Boaz is not interested in how he looks in Ruth's eyes as much as in

---

42. Younger, *Ruth*, 454; cf. Goldingay, *Ruth*, 171–72. "Specially you who are Christian men, I repeat it in your hearing,—be not less liberal than was the Jew; and if of old when there were types and shadows they left good gleanings for the poor; scatter ye with a liberal hand now that ye have come to the substance and the fulness of the gospel. Rob not the poor man of his little, but earn his blessing by your abundant generosity in the time of reaping your fields," (C. H. Spurgeon, *The Metropolitan Tabernacle Pulpit Sermons*, vol. 8 [London: Passmore, 1862], 447).

43. Webb, *Five Festive Garments*, 57.

genuinely helping her and Naomi."[44] How many of us can claim the same when helping others? In his comments on generosity, Jesus encouraged us not to let our left hand know what our right was doing when blessing and giving to others (Matt 6:3–4). Doing so will allow us to become mighty like Boaz, "and your Father who sees in secret will reward you" (Matt 6:4).

There is a beautiful shadow of Christ present in this chapter. Boaz showed compassion and generosity to Ruth, just as Jesus shows compassion and generosity to us. Just as Boaz spoke kindly to Ruth, Jesus speaks kindly to those ensnared in sin and sorrow. He lifts up our heads and invites us to labor in his fields under his wings of protection. Like Boaz, he insists we drink of his water so that we will thirst no more. Moreover, Christ, like Boaz, invites us to a meal where he serves us himself. That meal, known as Communion or the Lord's Supper, is where we are reminded of the tremendous grace Christ has extended to us. "The prodigal, who once fed upon husks, sits down to eat the bread of children. We, who were worthy to be esteemed as dogs, are here permitted to take the place of adopted sons and daughters."[45] In our sorrow and pain on the Bethlehem Road, occasions such as the Lord's Supper can be a weekly reminder that God still loves us, longs to fellowship with us, and has provided a means of doing so through Jesus' atonement at Golgotha. "Taste and see that the LORD is good! Blessed is the man who takes refuge in him!" (Ps 34:8).

As I contemplate Naomi and Ruth's plight as widows in an ancient culture, it occurs to me that their hope for a brighter future lay partly in God's revealed will—in his past revelations, and not just his future providence. In any ancient godless culture, childless widows often resigned themselves to slavery, prostitution, or death. Israel's God, however, had great concern for these vulnerable women (Deut 10:17–

---

44. Younger, *Ruth*, 453.

45. C. H. Spurgeon, *The Metropolitan Tabernacle Pulpit Sermons*, vol. 9 (London: Passmore, 1863), 424.

18; Pss 68:5; 146:9; Jer 49:11) and mandated their preservation (Exod 22:22–24; Deut 14:28–29; 24:17–20; 26:12–13; 27:19). Simply put, God had already put in place mechanisms (e.g. gleaning in the fields, the role of the *go'el* and *levir*) for the care of women just like Naomi and Ruth. In the midst of heartache and grief, we often ask, "Where is God?" We wonder why his providence has bypassed or failed us. I have found that God's presence is never more powerfully felt than in our obedience to his Word. This is also a call for the church, the body of Christ on earth, to be the answer to "Where is God?"[46] In a morally relative society (whether it be Israel during the Judges period, or our own in the 21st century), faithful and compassionate obedience to God's law might do more to spread the Good News than a thousand sermons. Arguably, the church of Christ never so adequately fulfills her charter as when she helps bear the burdens of others, "and so fulfill[s] the law of Christ" (Gal 6:2).

---

46. Philip Yancey, *Where Is God When It Hurts?* (Grand Rapids: Zondervan, 1990).

3

THE SECOND PEDAL

When I was about six, I received a brand new blue bicycle. I had already been learning how to ride a "big boy bike" for several months and, like every kid, I powered through the balance issues until I learned to propel the bike forward using the pedals. In no time at all, I was zipping around my grandparents' homestead like a young Evel Knievel.

As my awesome bike skills developed, I experimented with how far I could ride by pushing down on only one pedal, allowing my other foot to dangle freely in the wind. At this point, I wouldn't blame you for asking, "Why would you do a dumb thing like that?" It wasn't long before I learned why there are two pedals instead of one. A bicycle is designed to propel forward by the dual use of *both* pedals. You might get to the same destination using only one pedal, but it's much more difficult and will take you twice as long.

I once heard the relationship between divine sovereignty and human responsibility illustrated as two pedals of a bicycle. It is not a precise metaphor—you can't press it too far before it breaks down—but it's a nice way of explaining the enigmatic relationship between God's actions and our own.

In the story of Ruth, we see how God was at work in order to secure a brighter future for these two suffering widows. The Lord visited Israel and ended the famine, beckoning Naomi home. The Lord brought the widows to Bethlehem just as the harvest was beginning. The Lord directed Ruth to glean in Boaz's field, rather than someone else's. God's sovereign providence was certainly at work.

But in this chapter, "a central theme of the book appears, namely that human action is the vehicle for achieving divine blessing and the fullness of human community."[1] Naomi took the initiative to return home. Ruth took the initiative to follow her and to glean in the fields. Boaz took the initiative to show unmerited, unexpected kindness to Ruth. In other words, divine providence and human initiative, working together, propelled the story forward.

In this chapter, it is Naomi's initiative (coupled once again with God's sovereign grace) that moves things along. Ruth had gleaned in Boaz's fields for two months, but the harvest was ending. Boaz, too, seemed to be unaware or uncertain as to what his obligations were as a kinsman-redeemer to Naomi and Ruth. "What looked like a clear solution to their widowed situation seems to have died out. While the provision of food is significant to their immediate need and somewhat beyond, it does not solve the long-term problem of their destitute widowhood. What appeared to be a promising relationship has evaporated."[2] Naomi, therefore, decided to get involved and coached Ruth on what to do next. Had Naomi not done so, both women might have remained in their impoverished widowhood in perpetuity.

God's involvement in this rather bizarre scene is difficult to discern at first glance, but how else are we to explain Boaz acting just as Naomi predicted? How else are we to explain his very favorable response to Ruth's request? How else are we to explain the plan unfolding as successfully as it did, given its high probability of scandal or failure?

---

1. Sakenfeld, *Ruth*, 59.

2. Younger, *Ruth*, 450. "Unquestionably the major turning point in the book is Naomi's stratagem to induce Boaz to accept this obligation, even though he apparently is so distantly related that neither he nor others thought it immediately incumbent upon him," (LaSor, *Survey*, 612).

> The reader stands back in awe, wondering what has possessed [Ruth]. Here is a servant demanding that the boss marry her, a Moabite making the demand of an Israelite, a woman making the demand of a man, a poor person making the demand of a rich man. Was this an act of foreigner naïveté, or a daughter-in-law's devotion to her mother-in-law, or another sign of the hidden hand of God? From a natural perspective the scheme was doomed from the beginning as a hopeless gamble, and the responsibility Naomi placed on Ruth was quite unreasonable. But it worked![3]

It is certainly true that we sometimes run ahead of God and his providence, acting on the idea of "If I don't, it won't." In certain situations, the best thing we can do is to get out of God's way and let him direct events. God has no business being anyone's co-pilot.

There are also times, however, when God expects us to act,[4] to prove our faith by our works (Jas 2:17, 26)—"to put legs on our prayers," as my dad used to say. This may never be truer than on the Bethlehem Road. In our pain, loneliness, grief, or isolation, we often expect divine providence to show up on our doorstep as a gift-wrapped package, and when it doesn't, we feel as if God has forsaken us. Or, like Naomi, that he is out to get us. It would do us well, in those times, to remember that there is a second pedal on the bike, and that God gave us two feet.

RUTH 3:1–5

Since Boaz had yet to make a move on Ruth, Naomi decided to help things along. She desired "rest" for her daughter-in-law, i.e. "the security and tranquility that a woman in Israel longed for and expected to find

---

3. Block, *Ruth*, 692.

4. "Some Christians seem to be sitting down and waiting, throughout their entire lives, because they are always requiring God to show them more before they launch out and trust Him. It is possible to be so afraid of making mistakes that we do nothing," (Jackman, *Ruth*, 346).

in the home of a loving husband."[5] In other words, she wanted to secure Ruth's future by arranging her marriage to Boaz (cf. 1:9).[6] If Naomi died unexpectedly, Ruth would have been in a very precarious position as a Moabite widow in Israel. In this beautiful story, it is not just Ruth's dedication to Naomi that is celebrated, but also Naomi's loving concern for Ruth.

Before Naomi sent her daughter-in-law to Boaz, she gave a specific set of instructions. Ruth must first wash, perfume herself,[7] and don special clothes. There is considerable debate as to what type of clothes Ruth wore on this occasion, and for exactly what purpose. Some think Naomi was prompting Ruth to adorn herself as a bride so as to make clearer to Boaz what she was asking.[8] In fact, the sequence of bathing, perfume, and special clothes is known to have been a prelude to wedding ceremonies in ancient Babylon[9] and is well attested in the OT (cf. Song 1:3, 12–14; 4:11–16; Ezek 16:9–10). By drawing comparisons to 2 Sam 12:20, Block argues that Naomi was instructing Ruth to end her period of mourning as a widow.[10] But Sakenfeld counters this by pointing out, "David took these steps not after a period of mourning for the dead child but immediately after the baby died, once his pleading for the life of the child had come

---

5. Block, *Ruth*, 681.

6. "A significant theological point emerges here. Earlier Naomi had wished for these same things (1:8–9). Here human means (i.e., Naomi's plan) carry out something previously understood to be in Yahweh's province. In response to providentially given opportunity, Naomi began to answer her own prayer!" (Hubbard, *Book of Ruth*, 199).

7. "The perfume mentioned here consisted of scented oils that would have been commonly used at celebrations and other festive occasions. The scents were usually derived from imported plants," (Walton, *Bible Background*, 279).

8. "Apparently it was an Israelite but not a Moabite procedure, for Naomi had to explain to Ruth what she must do to show Boaz that she was interested in marriage with him," (Morris, "Ruth," 284).

9. S. Greengus, "Old Babylonian Ceremonies and Rites," *JCS* 20 (1966): 55–72. Contra Campbell, who believes the text is too ambiguous to indicate the purpose of the bathing, perfume, and special clothes (*Ruth*, 131).

10. Block, *Ruth*, 684.

to nought."[11] Perhaps these two concepts—termination of mourning and the desire for matrimony—are not mutually exclusive.

Prepared, Ruth went to the threshing floor to find Boaz. Following the barley and wheat harvests, the grain would be threshed in an area of hard-packed earth or smooth rock. The grain stalks would be tossed into the air with a fork, and "the wind blew the chaff and straw to the side, while the kernels which are heavier fell back directly to the floor,"[12] (cf. Hos 13:3). The grain would then be collected into piles. Threshing was often done during the evening breeze; when it had died down, threshing ended for the day, and the workers would celebrate with food and drink.[13] Since these fields and threshing floors could easily be a few miles from town, Boaz likely slept near the threshing floor to protect his valuable harvest from thieves.[14] Sleeping nearby also enabled workers to resume early the next morning when the breeze returned.

The most perplexing point, at least to modern readers, is that Naomi directed Ruth to "uncover his feet and lie down," and that Boaz would then know what to do. The command is disturbing because "feet" elsewhere in the OT is often a euphemism for genitals (e.g. Deut 28:57; Judg 3:24; 1 Sam 24:3; Isa 7:20; Ezek 16:25). Here, however, the Hebrew *margelot* is used, not *regalim* (the former is used 4x in Ruth 3 and once in Dan 10:6).[15] Simply put, it seems Ruth uncovered nothing more than Boaz's feet.

---

11. Sakenfeld, *Ruth*, 54.

12. Fuerst, *Ruth*, 22.

13. Eskenazi argues, "These terms suggest feasting, not merely an ordinary meal," (*Ruth*, 56). There was certainly a lot of joy, celebration, and feasting during the harvest season (cf. Isa 9:3; 41:14–16), and the fact that Boaz's "heart was merry" (3:7) may indicate that he had had too much to drink (cf. Esth 1:10), but not necessarily (cf. Judg 18:20; 1 Kgs 8:66; 21:7; Prov 15:15). Block notes an important distinction. "Although Boaz's 'drinking' probably included an alcoholic beverage, our passage makes no mention whatsoever of him getting drunk or of engaging in actions that he would not have done sober," (*Ruth*, 684).

14. Manor, "Ruth," 257.

15. In Dan 10, *margelot* is juxtaposed with "arms," meaning that *margelot* is "inclusive of feet, legs, and thighs. Accordingly, it seems Naomi is advising Ruth to uncover Boaz's lower limbs, probably exclusive of his genitals," (Block, *Ruth*, 686). He later says the narrator's choice

The scandal, unfortunately, is not dissipated so easily. A man and woman were still lying next to each other in the middle of the night, and "in the ancient world, to speak of a woman uncovering any part of a man's body at night (when that man is not her husband) was highly suggestive."[16]

Moreover, the Hebrew verb for "uncover" was often itself a euphemism for sexual activity (e.g. Lev 18:6–19, 20:11; Deut 22:30; 23:1; 27:20), and some argue that threshing time in ancient cultures was also a time of celebration with all the immoral revelry of Mardi Gras or Spring Break on South Padre (cf. Hos 9:1).[17] However, "the text of Ruth does not suggest a blatant sexual act but is provocative in its ambiguity."[18]

What are we to make of this strange scene?

RUTH 3:6–13

Some people think that a modern love story has to have at least one sex scene, but this is as close as we get to such an episode in the book of Ruth. As scandalous as Ruth's midnight visit might appear to be, Boaz and Ruth are to be commended that no illicit tryst took place.

Ruth did exactly as Naomi had instructed. She arrived at the threshing floor, waited for Boaz to hit the hay (perhaps literally in this case), quietly approached the sleeping landowner to uncover his feet, and then lay down beside him, presenting "herself as a humble petitioner seeking his

---

of *margelot* "actually draws the reader's attention away from the genitals and diffuses it over the limbs as a whole," (Ibid.).

16. Eskenazi, *Ruth*, 53.

17. "It seems that in this cultural context, at winnowing time the threshing floor often became a place of illicit sexual behavior. Realizing that the men would spend the night in the fields next to the piles of grain, prostitutes would go out to them and offer their services," (Block, *Ruth*, 685).

18. Walton, *Bible Background*, 279. One scholar lists seven different double entendres in Ruth 3 and argues that their "use was not an accident. The author purposefully uses them to increase tension," (Harry J. Harm, "The Function of Double Entendre in Ruth Three," *JOTT* 7 [1995]: 19–27). "That our author intends the explicitly sexual sense of 'uncover his genitals and lie down' is in my opinion utterly improbable," (Younger, *Ruth*, 459).

protection."[19] The narrator helps us appreciate how alarming this must have been to Boaz—"At midnight the man was startled and turned over, and behold, a woman lay at his feet!" (3:8).

Had Boaz been a cowboy in the Old West, he would have bolted upright with a pistol in hand, tempted to shoot first and ask questions later. There is nothing more unnerving than waking from a deep sleep to find someone sitting unexpectedly next to you (it is, after all, a common motif in horror films). You and I both know how disorienting those first few moments can be—"Who am I? Where am I? What's happened?" Imagine what Boaz must have thought when he awoke so suddenly. Were thieves attempting to steal his hard-earned grain? Had a wild animal approached—a lion or a bear, both of which Boaz's great-grandson David would one day kill (1 Sam 17:36), perhaps in these very fields?

Boaz demanded that this midnight stranger identify him/herself. Only then did Ruth speak, referring to herself as Boaz's servant and requesting that he spread his "wings" (i.e. his garment) over her as the go'el, or the kinsman-redeemer. Spreading the garment over someone was a marriage proposal in the ANE[20] (Deut 22:30; 27:20; Ezek 16:8; Mal 2:16), and is still practiced today by people in that part of the world.[21] It reflected the husband's vow to protect and provide for his wife, who sought refuge under his "wings." Of deeper significance is that Ruth repeated nearly verbatim the blessing/wish Boaz expressed at their first meeting

---

19. Hubbard, *Book of Ruth*, 204. Jamieson says, "Ruth lay crosswise at his feet—a position in which Eastern servants frequently sleep in the same chamber or tent with their master," (*Commentary*, 131).

20. Kruger notes several ancient parallels to the custom here in Ruth 3. For example, one divorce procedure in the ANE was for the husband to cut his wife's garment. In a related custom, women were often publicly stripped of their garments to shame them for their adultery (Paul A. Kruger, "The Hem of the Garment in Marriage: The Meaning of the Symbolic Gesture in Ruth 3:9 and Ezek 16:8," *JNSL* 12 [1984]: 79–86).

21. "To this day in many parts of the East, to say of anyone that he put his skirt over a woman, is synonymous with saying that he married her; and at all the marriages of the modern Jews and Hindus, one part of the ceremony is for the bridegroom to put a silken or cotton cloak around his bride," (Jamieson, *Commentary*, 132).

(2:12); Boaz had wished that God would reward Ruth for her seeking refuge under Yahweh's wings; here, Ruth petitions Boaz to embody that same protection by spreading his wings/garment over her. "By repeating the key word from his own lips, Ruth essentially asks Boaz to answer his own prayer!"[22]

We can't discount Ruth's courage in approaching Boaz in this manner. She followed Naomi's instructions at grave risk to herself, and we can only wonder if she truly understood the consequences of what she was doing.

> For example, Boaz could mock her request for marriage to him—a wealthy and powerful Israelite landowner— as a vain attempt at social climbing for a poor widowed "Moabitess." Or, since Ruth has not secured a new marriage contract and is technically still the wife of Mahlon (cf. 4:5, 10), Boaz could charge her with failing in her family responsibilities, branding her an adulteress. Or even worse, Boaz could use the night's opportunity for his sexual pleasure, bringing on her great humiliation, and then malign her (charging her with entrapment) or even charge her with prostitution.[23]

If anything in this story explicitly militates against this being a steamy sex scene, it is Boaz's response to Ruth's marriage proposal.[24] The reader already knows Boaz to be a mighty or worthy man (2:1)—a

---

22. Younger, *Ruth*, 462. "Their marriage was to be the means by which Yahweh protected Ruth and, at the same time, 'paid her in full' for her past kindnesses. Theologically, God worked here not by direct intervention but within righteous human acts," (Hubbard, *Book of Ruth*, 212). He adds, "In this case, the 'righteous human act' was Boaz's execution of his duty as *gō'ēl*. This suggests something further: God works through human obedience to his legal instructions," (Ibid., n. 35).

23. Younger, *Ruth*, 460.

24. "These are hardly the flippant words of one who has been seduced by a woman of the night. Again the reader is inclined to see the hidden hand of God guiding not only the actions of individuals but their reactions and their dispositions so that in the end Yahweh's agenda is fulfilled. Boaz's words have the ring of divine inspiration," (Block, *Ruth*, 692–93).

God-fearing, righteous man. We have already witnessed his honorable and generous actions towards Ruth and Naomi. Upon discovering that a young woman was lying beside him in the middle of the night, Boaz did not castigate her as a whore, nor did he accept Ruth's "advances" by ordering champagne and playing Barry White to set the mood. No, Boaz referred to her as a "worthy woman" (3:11; cf. Prov 31:10) and seemed to immediately understand what Ruth sought when she mentioned "wings" and "redeemer." Consistent with his character, Boaz responded with *hesed*.

When Ruth requested that Boaz spread his wings over her, she did so because she understood Boaz to be "a redeemer" (3:9). This is the second time that term has appeared in the book, the first being in 2:20; it occurs in Ruth a total of 9x as a noun, 12x as a verb. The Hebrew *gō'el* represented a kinsman-redeemer in Israelite society, one who used his own resources to help members of his clan when they were in need.

> As a kinship term it denotes the near relative who is responsible for the economic well-being of a relative, and he comes into play especially when the relative is in distress and cannot get himself/herself out of the crisis. . . . The Israelite provision for the *gō'el* is based upon an assumption of corporate solidarity and the sanctity of the family/clan: to offend a relative is to offend oneself. The custom of redemption was designed to maintain the wholeness and health of family relationships, even after the person has died.[25]

In the final chapter of Ruth, Boaz offered to accept the responsibilities of a *go'el* and redeem Naomi's land, fulfilling Lev 25:25—"If your brother

---

25. Block, *Ruth*, 674–75. He goes on to list five aspects of the *go'el* role: 1.) Keep property within the family/clan (Lev 25:25–30), 2.) Keep relatives out of slavery, buying their freedom if necessary (Lev 25:47–55), 3.) Hunt down and execute those who murder family members (Num 35:12, 19–27), 4.) Receive restitution on behalf of a deceased relative (Num 5:8), and 5.) See that justice is served in any lawsuit concerning a relative (Job 19:25; Ps 119:154; Jer 50:34) (Ibid., 674).

becomes poor and sells part of his property, then his nearest redeemer [*go'el*] shall come and redeem what his brother has sold." Remember that possessing land in Palestine was extremely important among the Israelites (cf. 1 Kgs 21:2–3). "Since Yahweh had granted the land to the Israelites as tenants, they could not sell it, and if they mortgaged a portion of it to pay debts, it was considered very important to regain ownership as soon as possible."[26]

What has puzzled scholars is how the *go'el* concept in Ruth seems to be intertwined with that of a *levir* (Latin for "brother-in-law"), one who accepted the responsibilities of levirate marriage.[27] While a kinsman-redeemer was a more distant relative who sought the good of his clan, a *levir* was a man who married his brother's widow in order to perpetuate the deceased's name (cf. Gen 38). "When a family died out physically, it ceased to exist metaphysically. That robbed Israel of one of her most prized possessions, namely, clan and tribal solidarity."[28] A *levir*, therefore, would marry his brother's widow, and the first child born to that union would be the legal heir of the deceased brother and would perpetuate his name (any other children would belong to the *levir*).

Elsewhere in the OT, marriage wasn't an actual part a *go'el*'s responsibilities, and a *levir* was not necessarily expected to assume the responsibilities of a *go'el*. Ruth seems to overlap the two by asking Boaz to marry her *because* he is a *go'el*, a kinsman-redeemer. Both a *go'el* and a *levir* were committed to the good of the clan, and if a family's bloodline died out, they would lose their stake in the Promised Land. Both of these losses would have been a terrible tragedy. So it was actually quite natural

---

26. Walton, *Bible Background*, 279. "Indeed, the ownership of the land of Israel is still the most explosive issue in the precarious balance of contemporary world politics, and the Bible tells us why," (Jackman, *Ruth*, 342).

27. For more on levirate marriage, see Dale W. Manor, "A Brief History of Levirate Marriage as It Relates to the Bible," *ResQ* 27 (1984): 129–42.

28. Younger, *Ruth*, 417.

for Ruth to intertwine the two positions[29]—a *go'el* helped the family by redeeming land; a *levir* by keeping the name of the deceased alive: "the 'redemption' of the land 'triggers,' so to speak, the levirate obligation."[30] Boaz also understood this; he not only expressed his willingness to marry Ruth and give her the security Naomi sought, but also his readiness to redeem the land (as we will discover in the next chapter).

However, as Boaz explained, there was another man who had dibs on redeeming Ruth and becoming her husband. The matter had to be discussed before Boaz and Ruth could be wed, but he promised that another sun would not set before he had seen the matter settled, swearing that he would do so "as the LORD lives" (3:13).[31]

In the meantime, he encouraged Ruth to rest beside him until the morning,[32] presumably because it would be shameful (cf. Song 5:7), not to mention dangerous, if Ruth were caught traveling at night. If she were seen returning to the city early in the morning with grain, people would have assumed she had been working overtime to secure food for herself and Naomi. Regardless, "Boaz's suggestion is a gesture of hospitality and protection—proving to Ruth (or to the reader) that he is indeed taking her under his wing."[33]

---

29. "The *go'el* custom, as reflected in Ruth, depicts an established custom wherein the redemption of property was merged with the practice of levirate marriage," (Josh Ketchum, "The Go'el Custom in Ruth: A Comparative Study," *ResQ* 52 [2010]: 237–45). Driesbach points out that Ruth likely did not use *go'el* in a technical way, "but simply a reference to a family member who should be concerned to resolve the bad situation of another." Since she was a Moabite and the *go'el* tradition seems to have been unique to Israel, Ruth may not have been familiar with how the tradition worked ("Ruth," 537).

30. Younger, *Ruth*, 403.

31. "By linking his promise to Yahweh's existence, Boaz willingly subjected himself to divine punishment if he failed to keep his word," (Hubbard, *Book of Ruth*, 219).

32. Boaz avoids any sexual inference to his invitation to spend the night by using the Hebrew word *lîn* (the same word Ruth used in 1:16), instead of *šākab* (Block, *Ruth*, 695). The former term is never used in Scripture in a sexual way.

33. Eskenazi, *Ruth*, 64.

I unapologetically confess that my taste in movies are those saturated with testosterone: *Braveheart, Gladiator, Rocky, Die Hard*, etc. Each has intense action sequences, battles, and explosions that get the adrenaline flowing. But among the (admittedly) very few chick flicks I've enjoyed is *Serendipity*, a film about two people who meet by chance in New York City but are then separated for many years. The girl scribbles her phone number inside the cover of a used book, thinking that if it is their destiny to end up together, then the guy will find the book, and they will reconnect and live happily ever after. Years later, on the cusp of their respective marriages to other people, they begin a fast-paced search for one another, and the plot drives the audience crazy with a multitude of near-encounters. The same thing happened in the U.S. sitcom *The Office*. Fans had to endure an excruciating three(!) seasons, wondering if Jim and Pam would ever get together. Goldingay reminds us that, "in any decent romantic comedy, ... there have to be threats to whether the couple do end up together; otherwise the movie will end too quickly."[34]

Personally, I'll stick with the explosions.

The book of Ruth is a romantic short story at its very best. We are given wonderful, well-rounded characters and the possibility of a relationship that will save Ruth and Naomi from poverty. Like so many other stories in this genre, the audience is left wondering if Boaz and Ruth will get together, or will some mysterious person or force foil this ancient romance? "From a story-telling point of view, this has the marvelous effect of creating one more suspenseful moment, in which Boaz is given his opportunity to show his worthiness; for it is one feature of Boaz's valor that he will not even usurp another man's right to act responsibly!"[35] From an audience's point of view, the suspense can be frustrating beyond belief!

34. Goldingay, *Ruth*, 180.

35. Campbell, *Ruth*, 137.

RUTH 3:14–18

Boaz tacitly acknowledged that this encounter with Ruth could have been perceived as a scandalous rendezvous when he prompted her to start for home before sunrise.[36] Not only did he want to preserve their good reputations; he was also "anxious not to jeopardize the legal matters of the following day by any shadow of immorality."[37] So in the morning, when there is just enough light to see, but not enough to recognize someone, Ruth made her way back to Bethlehem. She might not have arrived in town before everyone began going about their daily business, but she would have placed enough distance between herself and the threshing floor that no one would have suspected her of tawdry or lurid behavior.[38]

Before she left, Boaz gave Ruth a parting gift of six measures of barley. The exact amount is indeterminate (the Hebrew text doesn't even say "measure"), but it would have been a significant amount. Naomi interpreted it as a sign that Boaz "will not rest but will settle the matter" that very day (3:18). Block believes that the grain functioned as a down payment of the bride price due Naomi as Ruth's legal guardian. Such a gift was not meant to purchase Ruth as property, but was rather "a promise to prepare for the wedding in good faith and a pledge for the good behavior of the groom toward the bride in the meantime."[39] The giving of food as payment for a bride price was not unheard of in ancient times.[40] Whatever its purpose, the gift of grain also functions as a literary device—Naomi,

---

36. "Ruth's night-time initiative was certainly open to misinterpretation—Boaz's unwillingness (v. 14) to let it become public knowledge makes that clear," (Auld, *Ruth*, 272–73).

37. Walton, *Bible Background*, 280.

38. "A woman stirring in the early morning would attract less suspicion, since work traditionally began before daylight in the Arab villages. The first task of the day being grinding, Ruth, with her load of barley, would be a natural figure," (Gray, *Ruth*, 396).

39. Block, *Ruth*, 700. Once a bride price was paid, a couple was betrothed, and "from this point onwards, the marriage, though not yet consummated, was legally in force," (NIDOTTE 2:860).

40. Greengus, "Babylonian Marriage Ceremonies," 61.

who had come back to Bethlehem "empty," was now "full." Would Yahweh/
Boaz fill up her life in other ways?[41]

It is fair to assume that, "if Ruth and Boaz had been deprived of
sleep that night, no doubt the same was true of Naomi."[42] When Ruth
returned home that morning, Naomi immediately interrogated her like
any concerned mother. Her specific question/agenda is hard to discern.
"How did you fare, my daughter?" (ESV) is actually "Is that you, my
daughter?" when rendered more literally from the Hebrew (cf. KJV). Of
course, Naomi knew that it was Ruth. "What Naomi does not know is who
Ruth has become as a result of her daring nighttime meeting with Boaz.
Naomi's question expresses an anticipated transformation."[43] The rabbis
expressed Naomi's interrogation in even plainer terms: "She meant: 'Are
you still a virgin, or a married woman?' to which Ruth replied: 'A virgin'"
(Ruth Rabbah 7.4).

The chapter closes with all the expectation of an edge-of-the-seat
romantic roller coaster. What will happen next? How will the plight
of these widows be resolved? Will the guy get the girl? At this point, it
seems Naomi and Ruth have done all they can to ensure a safe future.
Everything now rests on Boaz. Will he live up to his promise? The tension
reminds us that sometimes, after we have done what is expected of us, we
simply must wait for God to act. We work to fulfill our responsibilities, to
push against the second pedal and move forward, but God has his own
timing, and we must learn to submit to and rest in it.

As I said before, providence is an odd thing. Just when you think that
God has stopped working on your behalf, something happens to humble
you and convict you that you have been on the Lord's mind all along. I'm

41. Hubbard, Book of Ruth, 229–30.

42. Block, Ruth, 699.

43. Eskenazi, Ruth, 67.

unsure of the direct relationship between divine providence and human action, but the story of Ruth affirms that God works *for* his people by working *in* and *through* them.

> It is through Boaz that God's kindness to Naomi and Ruth receives its content and meaning. God had provided food for Judah (1:6), but only through Boaz has God provided food for the two returning widows. In God's providence Ruth came to Boaz's field, but it is Boaz who looks kindly upon Ruth in her need. Divine loyalty takes shape in the community and in individual lives through human actions.[44]

In the same way, God's providence worked through Naomi's concern for Ruth's long-term security, in Ruth's boldness to follow through with Naomi's risky plan, and in Boaz's magnanimous acceptance of Ruth's proposal. Could God have found a way to bless Ruth, Naomi, and Boaz without their participation? Of course, but this isn't about what God is able or unable to do. Rather, it's about our acting as a second pedal, about our being an instrument of divine sovereignty, of knowing the rich blessing of being a conduit or vessel of God's redemption, deliverance, and healing for the brokenhearted.

In the end, there is just one question that matters: Will we allow the Lord to work through us and, thereby, know the blessing of being a blessing to others? It is only when we open ourselves up to his divine plan, after all, that our bicycle of faith moves forward along the Bethlehem Road. We push one pedal; God pushes the other.

---

44. Sakenfeld, *Ruth*, 48.

TALKING POINTS

O ur *hesed* must be willing to take risks. Ruth could have allowed the dangerous unknown to intimidate and prevent her from gleaning in the fields. She could have made excuses as to why Naomi's plan was too risky or would never work. After all, the threats were real. She also could have allowed herself to be immobilized by her own grief and sorrow. What if her reaction had been, "I have done more than was expected for my mother-in-law; now I'm going to wait for something good to happen to me." In the same way, Naomi took a risk in seeking a husband for Ruth—what if the Moabite widow forgot her mother-in-law after the wedding? Who would see to Naomi's needs in her old age? Ruth and Naomi's primary concern, however, was for one another, not themselves. Neither wanted to wait for a blessing to come to them, but rather sought to be a blessing to each other. Sometimes, we talk ourselves out of helping others—of showing them *hesed*—because the risks are too great, or because we think it's our turn to take a ride on the wheel of blessing. It is impossible, however, to pass on the love of Christ to others without personal cost, and if we are always seeking a blessing for ourselves, we miss the incredible opportunity to bless others—which is the greatest blessing of all (Acts 20:35).

I n the story, Boaz celebrates Ruth as a "worthy woman" (3:11), the same description used for the woman of Prov 31. John MacArthur draws several important parallels between these two righteous examples of Christ-glorifying womanhood. Both were devoted to their families (cf. Ruth 1:15–18; Prov 31:10–12). Both delighted in their work (cf. Ruth 2:2; Prov 31:13). Both were diligent in their labor (cf. Ruth 2:7, 17, 23; Prov 31:14–18, 19–21, 24, 27). Both were dedicated to godly speech (cf. Ruth 2:10, 13; Prov 31:26). Both exemplified a dependence on God (cf. Ruth 2:12; Prov 31:25, 30). Both exercised modesty and discretion around men (cf. Ruth 3:3, 6–13; Prov 31:11–12, 22–23). Finally, both were a blessing to others (cf. Ruth 4:14–15; Prov 31:28–29).[45] "O Lord, raise up more Ruths among your people!"

I certainly believe that we should avoid as many compromising situations as possible. Jesus prompted his followers to watch and pray that they not fall into temptation (Matt 26:41). But Jesus himself was tempted through no fault of his own. This tells me that in the natural course of living, we are inevitably placed in compromising, untenable situations. Thus, in addition to avoiding as many of these situations as possible, it is doubly important that we avoid developing a compromising character. When compromising circumstances and character mix together, the deadly toxin of sin is created, and spiritual death is the result. Boaz and Ruth's example is a powerful one. They found themselves in a compromising situation, but avoided sexual immorality because both their characters were noble. "In a world obsessed with taking advantage of every opportunity for personal gratification—rare indeed is the movie that shows characters in sexually charged circumstances not fulfilling their self-interest—we need encouragement that to act with integrity is not only possible but preferable."[46]

---

45. John MacArthur, *The MacArthur Study Bible* (Nashville: Nelson, 1997), 373.

46. Younger, *Ruth,* 468.

4

TOMORROW

Much like chick flicks, I'm not a huge fan of musicals, but I do like the Broadway hit *Annie*, which debuted in 1977. It's the story of a Depression-era, New York City orphan, who is tired of the "hard-knock life" at the orphanage and dreams of the day when she will be adopted by loving parents and given a home of her own.

In the meantime, when Annie wasn't trying to run away, she lived under the tyrannical rule of the orphanage's matron, the liquor-loving, little-girl-loathing, Miss Hannigan. Annie's life finally takes a fortuitous turn when the assistant to a local billionaire comes to the orphanage to invite a girl to spend a week at her employer's mansion. The rest of the musical focuses on the budding friendship between Annie and Oliver Warbucks, whose heart predictably softens to the little girl's innate charm. In the end, he adopts her, giving her the family and home she has always desired.

The musical's trademark song, "Tomorrow," is beloved by many, and for good reason. It expresses the hope of the downtrodden, namely that pain and suffering cannot last forever, that there will surely be a warm-and-fuzzy ending where everyone lives happily ever after. Most everyone loves a good rags-to-riches story, and *Annie* doesn't disappoint us.

Neither does the story of Ruth.

The first-time reader is taken on an emotional roller coaster. The narrative begins with tragedy, and just when the narrator seemingly resolves Naomi and Ruth's plight, the plot stalls. Just when we think Boaz and Ruth's nuptials are a done deal, he informs her that another kinsman-redeemer must first decline his responsibility. Fortunately for us, the plot does not linger—Boaz vowed to address the issue the next day, and he did just that.

The end of the story involves several quick scenes. Boaz and Ruth are married, and we can imagine the occasion was one of great joy in the little town of Bethlehem. Ruth, previously thought to be barren, becomes pregnant. A bouncing baby is born to Ruth and Boaz and, more importantly, to his adopted grandmother. Indeed, it is Naomi who occupies the spotlight in the final verses of the story. A widow who had returned empty to Bethlehem is now portrayed as "full" because of the faithfulness of her daughter-in-law.

For the first-time reader of Ruth's story, there is also a twist at the end of the narrative, a startling "I did *not* see that coming!" moment that leaves the audience smiling. Such a twist proves two things. First, our suffering is always part of God's grander plan to unite all things in heaven and on earth. Just as Job had no clue the part he played in a bout of cosmic warfare, so too are we ignorant as to exactly what is at stake as we travel the daunting and difficult Bethlehem Road.

Second, the faithfulness of Ruth, Naomi, and Boaz to one another, even in random or seemingly unimportant ways, had eternal consequences. In *Annie*, a small act of kindness by a wealthy billionaire changed more than the life of a little orphan—it transformed Oliver Warbucks' heart and entire household. As we will discover, the *hesed* of Boaz, Naomi, and Ruth—combined with God's mysterious hand of providence—changed the destiny of the whole world. We never know the hope we give "Tomorrow" by the *hesed* we show today.

RUTH 4:1–12

Just as he had promised Ruth and Naomi, Boaz wasted no time before addressing the legal barriers standing in the way of matrimony. He practically made a beeline for Bethlehem's city gates. In ancient times, city gates functioned as a city hall or courthouse square of sorts[1] (cf. Josh 20:4; 2 Sam 15:2; Prov 22:22; 31:23). "Merchants, visitors, messengers and judges all frequented that area and conducted their business there. It was a logical place to find someone you might be looking for."[2]

Boaz knew the town elders[3] would be drinking their morning coffee at the city gate (cf. Deut 21:19; 22:15; 25:7; Lam 5:14). Moreover, the man with whom Boaz needed to discuss the matter would have to pass through the gate on his way to work. The narrator says, "Behold, the redeemer, of whom Boaz had spoken, came by" (4:1), as if this is just one more moment of divine providence disguised as random happenstance. The narrator is affirming that God, who had been orchestrating events up to this point, remained very much on top of the situation. It would be his mysterious hand that would direct the legal proceedings about to unfold.[4]

Obscure in English translations, but evident in the Hebrew text, is the way in which Boaz referred to this mystery man. He did not call him

---

1. Hubbard suggests that "to go up to the gate" is the same idiomatically as our own "to go to court" (*Book of Ruth*, 231, n. 1).

2. "Numerous excavations have produced gate plans showing that often there were benches lining the whole area where people could meet for their various purposes. Since only limited excavation has been done at Bethlehem, no gate from this period has yet been uncovered," (Walton, *Bible Background*, 280). Since Bethlehem's gate was likely smaller than average, Block thinks the proceedings took place in a plaza just inside the gate (*Ruth*, 707).

3. The number of city elders is not mentioned, but we know there were more than ten (4:2) and Succoth had 77 in Gideon's time (Judg 8:14). Manor ("Ruth," 258–59) notes that the Hebrew term translated "elder" is derived from the word meaning "beard," and thus noted someone of advanced age—but presumably someone who could still buy green bananas. The authority of the city elders "extended to murder trials (Deut. 19:12; 21:1–9; Josh. 20:4), disputes over virginity (Deut. 22:15), asylum (Deut. 19:11–12; Josh. 20:1–6), and levirate marriage (Deut. 25:5–10). "In this case, they were called upon to ratify the settlement of family redemption rights," (Hubbard, *Book of Ruth*, 235).

4. "Commentators who point out that virtually every male in town was bound to go out through the gate at some time during the morning on the way to work in the field are missing the impact of the Hebrew construction, which at least in Gen 24:15 and in Ruth conveys a hint of God's working behind the scenes," (Campbell, *Ruth*, 141).

"friend" (4:1), but essentially acknowledged him as Mr. "So and So," a moniker not that different from our own "John Doe." The Hebrew uses a stock phrase deliberately intended to obscure the person's identity (cf. 1 Sam 21:2; 2 Kgs 6:8). It's popularly thought that the narrator omitted the closer kinsman's name as a "way of pronouncing a condemnation upon him for withdrawing from his (levirate/*go'el*) responsibilities."[5]

After Boaz and the unnamed kinsman had taken their seats in the presence of the Bethlehem elders, Boaz explained the situation. He told the man that Naomi was selling the property previously belonging to her late husband, Elimelech (4:3). It is a simple enough statement, yet it has confused some scholars for several reasons: Why has the narrator not mentioned this land sooner? If Naomi owned land, why had she and Ruth been forced to glean in the fields like paupers? Women could not own land in the ANE, so how could Naomi sell it? How was redeeming Elimelech's land connected at all to marrying Ruth?[6]

There have been several attempts to reconstruct the legal situation that Boaz alludes to in his opening statement. The most plausible solution is that Elimelech, before moving to Moab, had sold the rights to his land to someone outside the family. This suggestion would explain why Naomi and Ruth could not sell the land and live off the proceeds. Naomi, now a penniless widow, was actually seeking a family member to buy back the land on her behalf and restore it to the clan (cf. Num 27:9–11; Jer 32:6–12). Boaz was offering his anonymous kinsman the opportunity to do so,[7] and it seems this man was eager to accept.

---

5. Hamilton, *Handbook*, 199. A majority of commentators castigate this mystery man for eschewing his *hesed* responsibilities, but I agree with Eskenazi: "The narrator portrays the unnamed redeemer as an ordinary, decent person, not as a villain. Like Orpah, he seeks to do the right thing but eventually gives up, thereby serving as a foil for the greater magnanimity of the story's heroes," (*Ruth*, 78; cf. Hubbard, *Book of Ruth*, 247).

6. "So interlocked are the problems here, and so full of uncertainties, that the literature on the topic may fairly be described as chaotic, with no two scholars in significant agreement with each other over the full range of issues," (Sakenfeld, *Ruth*, 70).

7. "Nowhere does the text suggest that Naomi had contacted Boaz to arrange for the legal

The sale of this property by Naomi would not have been permanent. Once the Year of Jubilee rolled around (Lev 25:14–16), the land would revert back to Elimelech's family—in this case, his heir via levirate marriage. "This arrangement helped keep Israel's wealth evenly distributed, and it meant that land-sale deals were actually more like long-term leases."[8] Naomi was not offering permanent rights to the land, but usufruct rights, which allowed the buyer to enjoy the use of the land until the next Jubilee year.[9]

The land, however, was a mere decoy. The real issue was who had the right to marry Ruth. For one thing, the price of the land is never mentioned.[10] That's because this passage is concerned with a person, not property. When the anonymous relative finally learned that the land went hand-in-hand with matrimony to Ruth (4:6), he suddenly developed cold feet. He never elaborated as to why, but it seems he was unwilling to marry Ruth because he might father a legal heir to Mahlon's name, as the law of levirate marriage dictated. If the deal had only entailed assuming responsibility for Naomi, the man would have willingly fulfilled his obligation. He likely knew the value of the land, reasoned that Naomi couldn't live forever, and was willing to care for the aged widow if it meant obtaining the deed to the property. The land would have been his in perpetuity once Elimelech's family died out, even beyond the next Jubilee.[11]

---

transfer of the rights. Nevertheless he seems to have concluded from the events of the previous night that he must do something about the land; it is not right for it to remain in an outsider's hands. Even though his conversation with Ruth at the threshing floor had not mentioned land at all, he knew that gaining the rights to the use of Naomi's property was the key to winning the right to Ruth's hand," (Block, *Ruth*, 710–11).

8. MacArthur, *Twelve Extraordinary Women*, 83.

9. Block, *Ruth*, 709–10; TDOT 8:292.

10. Eskenazi, *Ruth*, 75.

11. "One can easily imagine him smiling to himself at his good fortune. For very little money, he could carry out a respected family duty and perhaps enhance his civic reputation. Financially, the investment was a bargain without risk. There were no known heirs of Elimelech to reclaim title to the property later, and elderly Naomi was certainly unlikely to produce any. Even the Year of Jubilee (Lev. 25:13–17), were it applicable, would pose no threat to his ownership. Hence, his little investment would develop into years of productive, profitable harvests; it would

Buying the land was an attractive opportunity, but when Ruth was suddenly part of the deal, he realized the birth of an heir would cost him the land because it would belong to the child, Mahlon's legal heir. The kinsman "was unwilling to have the family portfolio split between his existing children and the potential offspring of a union with Ruth."[12] Indeed, the man's use of "impair" (ESV) or "endanger" (NIV) in 4:6 invokes the idea of financial ruin. It is used elsewhere in the OT to describe the catastrophic effects of war (2 Chr 34:11) and insect infestation (Mal 3:11). As far as the kinsman was concerned, this was a bad investment opportunity, so he passed on it.[13]

What follows is an odd scene.[14] The note of 4:7 indicates that this custom had already passed into the history books by the time Ruth's story was written down. Instead of shaking hands or signing on the dotted line, real estate transactions were sealed in ancient Israel by removing the sandal and passing it to the other party.

Other real estate transactions in the ANE reflect similar practices. At Nuzi, it was the custom that, "to make the transfer of real estate more valid, a man would 'lift up his foot from his property' and 'placed the foot of the other man in it.'"[15] When God swore to make Canaan the legal property of Abraham and his descendants, he commanded the patriarch to walk the land's boundaries (Gen 13:17). Elsewhere in antiquity, real estate transfers were not considered valid until the new owner had stepped foot on the

---

enlarge the inheritance of his heirs. How could he lose?" (Hubbard, *Book of Ruth*, 242).

12. *MacArthur, Study Bible*, 372.

13. There is also the possibility, however remote, that this man had no interest in marrying Ruth since she was a foreigner; this was the speculation of at least one rabbi (*Ruth Rabbah* 7.7).

14. Some try to tie this scene to Deut 25, but there are several differences; particularly, "There is no sense in this passage [in Ruth] that the next of kin is humiliated by this exchange," (Victor H. Matthews, *Judges and Ruth* [Cambridge: Cambridge Univ. Press, 2004], 240).

15. Ernest R. Lacheman, "Note on Ruth 4 7–8," *JBL* 56 (1937): 53. He later adds, "It is logical to conclude that this expression which had at first only a legal meaning developed into a symbolical meaning. Then the biblical tradition took a further step. The 'lifting up of the foot' became more concrete and real with the 'pulling off of the shoe,'" (Ibid., 56).

property; several OT passages reflect this (cf. Deut 1:36; 11:24; Josh 1:3; 14:9). All of these examples might have been part of a broader belief that one's feet or shoes "symbolized power, possession, and domination" (cf. Josh 10:24; Pss 8:6; 60:8).[16] Thus, when the kinsman removed his sandal and gave it to Boaz, he was actually submitting to the latter. Boaz was, as of that moment, the rightful owner of Elimelech's land and Ruth's hand.

Having obtained rights to all that was Elimelech's, Boaz testified that he had done so "to perpetuate the name of the dead in his inheritance, that the name of the dead may not be cut off from among his brothers and from the gate of his native place" (4:10). In ancient Israel, one's "name" was more than the moniker they went by; it represented a person's very essence. "One of the most fearful curses one person could invoke on another [in the ancient world] was 'May your seed perish and your name die out,'"[17] (cf. 1 Sam 24:21; 2 Sam 14:7). In lieu of a belief that the righteous went to heaven and the wicked went to hell, "an Israelite's afterlife depended upon having descendants living on ancestral soil. Without them, he ceased to exist."[18]

The scene ends with the citizens of Bethlehem pronouncing a proper blessing on Boaz and Ruth. As you can tell, the blessing had less to do with romance and more to do with children (cf. Gen 17:16; 24:60); this explains the echoing of the names of Rachel (who had ties to Bethlehem, Gen 35:19), Leah, and Tamar. It was crucial that every marriage produce children in order to perpetuate the existence of the family, clan, and, most

---

16. Hubbard, *Book of Ruth*, 251. He goes on to mention, "When Moses removed his shoes (Exod. 3:5; cf. Josh. 5:15), he acknowledged Yahweh's lordship; when David walked barefoot, he showed his powerlessness and humiliation (2 Sam. 15:30; cf. Isa. 20:2–4; Ezek. 24:17,23)," (Ibid.).

17. Block, *Ruth*, 714–15. He later adds, "The ancients believed that when a person's name is never mentioned after his death, he ceases to exist (Isa 14:20)," (Ibid., 723).

18. Hubbard, *Book of Ruth*, 244. He adds, "Even today, Jews annually read the names of the dead at a synagogue service to emphasize their continued presence among the living," (Ibid., n. 45).

importantly, the tribes of Israel, since more children served as a defense against Israel's enemies (Ps 127:3–5).

The reference to Perez, Tamar, and Judah (Gen 38) is particularly noteworthy. These stories both concerned a Gentile widow without an heir who chose "to approach an older man in a socially unacceptable way in order to effect a change in the situation. Most likely it is especially this last point that leads to the inclusion of the reference to Judah and Tamar in Ruth."[19] More significantly, both these women are later mentioned in the genealogy of Christ (Matt 1:3, 5). If God had blessed Judah in spite of his unfaithfulness to Tamar, how much more would Yahweh bless Boaz, who had shown remarkable *hesed* to Ruth and Naomi!

RUTH 4:13–16

We can expect that Boaz and Ruth's ceremony[20] was unlike any other wedding Bethlehem had seen, at least in quite a while. I like to imagine that the entire community turned out for the event and reveled in the joy of what Yahweh had done to preserve a family from extinction, and in how he had rewarded this Moabite widow for her faithfulness.

Yahweh's blessing on this marriage did not end with the bouquet toss— we are led to believe that Ruth became pregnant almost immediately as a direct result of God's intervention: "So Boaz took Ruth, and she became his wife. And he went in to her, and the LORD gave her conception, and she bore a son" (4:13). After a decade of marriage to Mahlon, she had failed to produce a child. Now, however, God was providentially at work, just as he had been with Sarah, Rebekah, Leah, and Rachel (and later, Hannah). "By granting Ruth motherhood, he finally paid the 'full wages' which her devotion to Naomi, both earlier and later (2:11; 3:10), had earned."[21]

---

19. Sakenfeld, *Ruth*, 78. For more on the connection between Tamar and Ruth, see Nielsen, *Ruth*, 95–99; Ellen van Wolde, "Texts in Dialogue with Texts: Intertextuality in the Ruth and Tamar Narratives," *BibInt* 5 (1997): 1–28.

20. "What was Boaz before he got married? Ruth-less!" That joke never gets old!

21. Hubbard, *Book of Ruth*, 267.

Indeed, this entire passage resonates with the truth that children are a great blessing from the Lord (cf. Pss 127–128). Since *Roe v. Wade* in 1973, more than 50 million unborn children have been aborted in the U.S. alone. We may have lost our ability to value each child as a precious blessing from heaven. Conception and birth are not haphazard biological events, but rather evidence of God's grace and skill as the Creator of all things (Ps 139:13). There are no unplanned pregnancies in heaven.

At the birth, the women of Bethlehem gathered around Naomi to congratulate her. How far this widow had come in the past year! She had returned to the house of bread, complaining of being empty because God was against her. Now her neighbors embraced her with joy and reminded Naomi that Yahweh had not abandoned her, but had blessed her with a redeemer.[22] For the rest of her life, Naomi would have a living reminder in Obed, her grandson, that God had turned her heartache into a "Hallelujah!"

Obed is also called Naomi's "restorer of life." Elsewhere in the OT, the phrase is used of bringing someone back from the brink of death (Job 33:30), or giving food to a starving man (Lam 1:11, 19). A few years ago, a severe illness prevented me from eating or drinking anything, even water, for more than three days. I remember how much better I felt after just a few bites of Jell-O! How much more grateful and refreshed did this Bethlehem widow feel with a grandson in her lap! Naomi was experiencing what David later sang about—"[The LORD] restores my soul" (Ps 23:3; cf. 19:7).

Naomi became Obed's "nurse," but don't mistake this to mean that she was a wet-nurse (she was likely too old to breastfeed), nor did Naomi formally adopt Obed (women in antiquity were likely unable to do so). In becoming his nurse, Naomi was the one primarily responsible for

---

22. In the natural course of reading this passage, it's easy to assume that "redeemer" (4:14) is a reference to Boaz. But scholars point out that the Hebrew term grammatically points back to Obed. In other words, Naomi's neighbors considered Obed, not Boaz, to be Naomi's true redeemer. Boaz was a much older man than Ruth, and if he died before Naomi, she now had another male to care for her in her old age (cf. Block, *Ruth*, 727–28; Eskenazi, *Ruth*, 89–90).

raising and nurturing little Obed (cf. 2 Kgs 10:1, 5; Esth 2:7). Note that the women say, "A son has been born to Naomi" (4:17), not to Ruth. In one sense, Obed didn't belong to Boaz or Mahlon or Elimelech, or even his mother. He was Naomi's! Every grandmother knows exactly what that means. This child was her legacy, a connection to her lost sons. For her part, Naomi does not speak in this scene. The surreal blessing likely left her speechless in a fog of gratitude and tears of joy. "Amid the loud celebration of the neighbor women, Naomi has no lines; she simply holds the baby close—she will love and nurture him as her own son."[23]

Furthermore, it is the women of Bethlehem who name Obed[24]—the the only time in the OT that someone other than the parents names a child. Surprisingly, however, this is not the most unconventional detail of the passage. The most startling statement by Naomi's neighbor is when Ruth is said to have been "more to you than seven sons" (4:15), thereby giving "the strongest possible cultural expression of her worth in a society that placed such great value upon male offspring,"[25] (cf. 1 Sam 1:8; 2:5; Job 1:2; 42:13). A woman with seven sons was considered blessed beyond measure, since a son ensured her security in old age—the main thing that had been stolen from Naomi when Mahlon and Chilion died. It was Ruth's faithfulness that bore fruit in the form of a surrogate grandson for Naomi. When we consider the lineage perpetuated by Ruth, we realize Naomi's neighbors spoke greater truth than even they knew.

RUTH 4:17–22

At the end of the passage, the narrator (presumably with a knowing grin on his face) introduces "the twist," the "Oh, wow!" moment that

23. Driesbach, "Ruth," 547.

24. "From a canonical-historical perspective, the name Obed ('Servant') should be interpreted as Ruth's final renunciation of Judges' self-absorbed narcissism," (Moore, "Ruth," 370).

25. Sakenfeld, *Ruth*, 82. "What more appropriate way to praise Ruth than to say she is worth seven times what the story has made such an absorbing concern—a son!" (Campbell, *Ruth*, 168).

a first-time reader never sees coming. Up until this point, the story of Ruth has had all the markings of a nice Once-upon-a-time fairy tale—a family is in grave distress, but they live happily ever after because the main characters are noble and virtuous. "Suddenly," however, "the simple, clever human story of two struggling widows takes on a startling new dimension. It becomes a bright, radiant thread woven into the fabric of Israel's larger national history."[26] The narrator informs us that Obed's grandson was David.

Yes, *that* David. The guy who threw down against the giant Goliath. The guy who made Saul look like an amateur puppet king. The guy who took Israel from a confederacy of tribes scarcely able to defend herself against her enemies, to a stable and secure empire, rivaled by no one and feared by everyone. The guy who wrote half of Israel's hymnal, who would dance before the Lord in worship with every ounce of energy he possessed, who was remembered as a man after God's own heart. The guy who cast such an incredible shadow over history that the promised Messiah was celebrated as the coming Son of David. The guy who, even now, has seen his star become the symbol of the modern nation of Israel and Jews around the world.

That David might not have been born had it not been for the story of Ruth. It is a reminder that in the course of leading quiet lives, of being a small light in the darkness, of embodying and spreading the holiness and love of God—the Lord is capable of taking obscure faithfulness and making it a crucial part of his great plan. Only eternity will know the good we do when we live a life that glorifies God.[27]

The final verses of Ruth are a brief genealogy, which is a surprising detail since biblical books typically do not end in this manner. The genealogy, however, functions as a "Now you know the rest of the story."

---

26. Hubbard, *Book of Ruth*, 277.

27. "During a period when many people did what was right in their own eyes, there were at least three who did what was right in God's eyes. It was through their faithfulness to God and to each other that God provided the Messiah for the world," (Arnold, *Encountering*, 193).

It also ties the entire book to the narratives in Genesis, where genealogies abound. Just as God had providentially orchestrated events in the lives of the patriarchs, he had likewise held sovereign sway over events in Ruth. In other words, genealogies are meant to remind us that God works out his purposes through multiple generations and across the centuries. "Limited as we are to one lifetime, each of us sees so little of what happens. A genealogy is a striking way of bringing before us the continuity of God's purpose through the ages. The process of history is not haphazard. There is a purpose in it all. And the purpose is the purpose of God."[28]

Regardless of when the book of Ruth was written down, this genealogy would have encouraged Israel to hope and trust in God, who graciously and sovereignly preserved the royal lineage through the dark days of the Judges period. In the midst of abject moral darkness and political turmoil, two righteous Israelites and a Moabite convert lived out the timeless principles of *hesed*, and thereby unwittingly became instruments of the divine plan.

> But the narrator could not know what implications the piety of these characters would have on generations of his own people that would come after him. If only he could have known that in the glorious providence of God the *hesed* of Boaz, Ruth, and Naomi would have laid the groundwork for the history of salvation that extends far beyond his own time and place. For as the genealogy of Matthew 1 indicates, one greater than David comes from the loins of Boaz. In the dark days of the judges the foundation is laid for the line that would produce the Savior, the Messiah, the Redeemer of a lost and destitute humanity.[29]

---

28. Morris, "Ruth," 318.

29. Block, *Ruth*, 737.

In the ANE, the seventh name in a genealogical list was a place of honor (cf. Enoch in Gen 5). So it shouldn't surprise us that Boaz occupies this most important position. What is surprising, however, is that Obed is reckoned as Boaz's son and not Mahlon's (cf. 4:9). Perhaps it is because of Boaz's faithfulness in the story that "authentic lines of blood have won out over legal fiction."[30] The tenth place, also a position of honor, belongs to David. If we compare this passage with 1 Chr 2, we discover that there are gaps in this genealogy. Apparently, the narrator was not interested in providing a strictly linear family tree. For example, Nahshon appears to be Boaz's grandfather and David's great-great-great-grandfather, but Nahshon lived during Moses' time (Exod 6:23). There are either gaps in the lineage, or we are to reckon sixty years to a single generation!

There is one last detail to observe in these final lines, one that most Christians miss, but that any faithful Israelite would notice immediately. If the offspring of Moabites were to be excluded from the assembly of the Lord until the tenth generation (Deut 23:3), how was David accepted when he was only Ruth's great-grandson? What hope did this shepherd boy have of dwelling in the house of the Lord forever (Ps 23:6) when his great-grandmother's ethnicity disqualified him? There have been many debates over this—scholarly and theological—that have produced several possible answers. Only one, however, makes complete and total sense:

Grace.

Who is truly worthy of the Lord's presence? Not Boaz the faithful, nor Naomi the doubter; not Ruth the Moabite, nor you, nor me. Paul said as much:

> And you were dead in your trespasses and sins in which
> you previously walked according to the ways of this

---

30. Ibid., 736.

world, according to the ruler who exercises authority over the lower heavens, the spirit now working in the disobedient. We too all previously lived among them in our fleshly desires, carrying out the inclinations of our flesh and thoughts, and we were by nature children under wrath as the others were also. But God, who is rich in mercy, because of His great love that He had for us, made us alive with the Messiah even though we were dead in trespasses. You are saved by grace! Together with Christ Jesus He also raised us up and seated us in the heavens, so that in the coming ages He might display the immeasurable riches of His grace through His kindness to us in Christ Jesus. For you are saved by grace through faith, and this is not from yourselves; it is God's gift— not from works, so that no one can boast.

Eph 2:1–9 HCSB

Later, Paul spoke of how Christ at the cross destroyed the dividing wall of hostility that prevented Gentiles from being in God's presence. It is because of Christ's atonement that God welcomes us all into his presence with open arms (Eph 2:11–17). Like Ruth and David, we know the Lord's goodness because of his faithful love—his *hesed*—towards us. Through Christ, there is infinite grace on the Bethlehem Road, and we can take comfort with David in singing joyously, "Surely goodness and mercy shall follow me all the days of my life, and I shall dwell in the house of the LORD forever."

TALKING POINTS

Boaz's refusal to take shortcuts to get what he wanted is a sterling example of the faithfulness God expects of us. Boaz was a man who loved God, and thus loved God's Law enough to obey it to the best of his ability. Even in this case where the Law itself wasn't clear, Boaz exhibited submission to the spirit of the law, "rather than scheme to circumvent it. Personal preference gave way to the prior rights of other relatives."[31] Yet some Christians today pay lip service to biblical authority, only to treat God's revealed will as a Sunday brunch buffet line. They make a big deal out of Jesus' teaching on divorce and remarriage (Matt 19:3–9), but aren't quite as passionate about the Lord's instruction on reconciliation (Matt 18:15–17).[32] Other churches will speak out boldly against homosexuality, but refuse to discipline adulterers in their midst. We need more men like Boaz, and women like Ruth, who love God's law and seek to obey it, regardless of the cost. We need to eschew short cuts and stop picking and choosing the laws we like, while ignoring those we do not.

Returning once more to the enigmatic relationship between divine sovereignty and human responsibility, this final chapter in Ruth's story provides us with a powerful reminder of just who deserves credit for blessings. The story would certainly not have turned out as it did were it not for Ruth, Naomi, and Boaz's mutual faithfulness and initiative. Yahweh, however, is the one who gets the credit in this chapter and rightly so. It is he who causes the unnamed kinsman to happen by the city gate. It is he who prompts the man to decline his claim, paving the way for Boaz and Ruth to marry. It is he who opens up Ruth's womb and blesses her with a son. These moments of seeming coincidence and good fortune are in fact flashing neon lights exalting God's intervention in even the most mundane moments of our lives. He is always deserving of our praise and

---

31. Hubbard, *Book of Ruth*, 217.

32. Younger, *Ruth*, 489.

gratitude for the good things that happen in life. Even when we wake up in the morning, we should attribute it to God's sovereign good pleasure and kindness towards us (cf. 1 Sam 2:6).

It is not coincidence that this story takes place during the Judges period, a time when "there was no king in Israel. Everyone did what was right in his own eyes (Judg 21:25). In Ruth's opening verses, we are introduced to a man whose name meant "God is my king," only to see him tragically perish outside of the Promised Land. In that moment, even the most faithful among us might despair! At the end of the story, however, we learn that Boaz and Ruth became the great-grandparents of Israel's greatest king.[33] God had brought everything full circle. Perhaps, then, the story of Ruth should make us pause and contemplate who is king of our lives. Do we, like so many Israelites in Judges, seek to do what is right in our own eyes? Do we enjoy being little sovereigns? Or have we bowed in submission and worship before the throne of Christ? Our own post-modern world is a lot like the one of Judges—full of gluttony, narcissism, and moral relativism. It is thus all the more imperative for others to see Christ reigning as king in our hearts, and that we become humble instruments of God's mysterious providence. When we finally see even the worst circumstances as opportunities for Jesus' glory, then we can know, once and for all, that he is reigning in our hearts and look forward to a brighter tomorrow.

---

33. Bezalel Porten, "The Scroll of Ruth: A Rhetorical Study," *Gratz College Annual* 7 (1978): 24–25.

EPILOGUE

More than a thousand years after Obed's birth, another baby was born in Bethlehem. As in Ruth's day, there was no king in Israel, but that was because Rome was now in charge, and Caesar Augustus was the Emperor. This same Augustus decreed a census be taken across the Roman Empire, so a Galilean carpenter named Joseph made the journey "to Judea, to Bethlehem the town of David, because he belonged to the house and line of David" (Luke 2:4 NIV). While Joseph was in town, his wife, Mary, gave birth to a baby boy. That child, a descendant of Boaz and Ruth, went on to become the Lion of Judah, the Righteous Branch, the King of kings, and the Savior of the world.

But even Jesus had to walk his own Bethlehem Road: the Via Dolorosa, the path that led from Jerusalem to Golgotha. Bethlehem lies only a few miles south of Jerusalem, and Jesus might have been able to see that little town in the distance as he hung upon the cross... at least until the entire world became engulfed in foreboding blackness.

The promise of the cross and the promise of Ruth's story is that our lives have meaning and purpose beyond our wildest imaginations. What we believe to be a hopeless tragedy, God often transforms into unprecedented triumph. The Lord used the darkest day in human history to bring about the forgiveness of sins and the salvation of the world. He knew in advance that wicked people would crucify his righteous son. As the apostle Peter testified to the crowd at Pentecost, "This man was handed over to you by God's deliberate plan and foreknowledge; and you, with the help of wicked men, put him to death by nailing him to the cross. But God raised him from the dead, freeing him from the agony of death, because it was impossible for death to keep its hold on him" (Acts 2:23–24 NIV).

Let that sink in for a moment. God knew in advance about the world's worst day, yet he providentially worked it for our good and his glory. When the Father was most *silent*, he was not *absent* (cf. Rev 5:9). Jesus' death was the Father's deliberate plan, and if the God of Israel can redeem the cross, then nothing can happen in your life or mine that he cannot redeem.

The cross is where Jesus atoned for our sins so that "there is therefore now no condemnation for those who are in Christ Jesus" (Rom 8:1). No longer do we have to wonder if God is out to get us, if his hand has gone out against us. "When Christ absorbs the wrath of God that we deserved, God never aims at our destruction but only at our holy, eternal happiness."[1]

In fact, Jesus' redemption of sin and suffering is where Ruth's story and our own so closely intersect. We all are in need of a redeemer. What Boaz was to Ruth, Jesus is to us. Once lowly foreigners with no claim to kindness or mercy, Christ now calls us "brothers" (Heb 2:11) and invites us to partake of every spiritual blessing (Eph 1:3). In the spirit of *hesed*, he shelters his bride—the church—in the shadow of his wings (Eph 5:25–27).

Most of all, Jesus rescued us from the kingdom of darkness and gave us hope for a better tomorrow. All of us have tried to live as little sovereigns, as masters over our own kingdoms. But Jesus saves us from such a ridiculous fairy tale, inviting us instead to cast our crowns before his throne and submit to his dominion and rule.

When we bow before Christ's throne, part of what we surrender is the fantasy that life will never be difficult, the fantasy that we will never experience pain (cf. 2 Tim 3:12). We also acknowledge at Christ's throne

---

1. Piper, *Sweet and Bitter Providence*, 136.

that he is in sovereign control of all things, that he knows best, and that he alone merits our total faith and trust. As Abraham Kuyper once declared, "There is not an inch in the whole area of human existence of which Christ, the sovereign of all, does not cry, 'It is mine!'"[2]

I have lived long enough to discover that life is not about having every dream come true, every want fulfilled, or every need met. Life is about glorifying God in all things. As long as we are focused on ourselves, our suffering will always be bitter. But when we are able to see the Bethlehem Road for what it is—an opportunity to glorify God and minister to others—we'll discover that our burdens are more bearable.

My heart has ached every day since my dad died, yet God has given me many opportunities to help other people in ways that would not have been possible were my dad still alive. Does that make my father's death "worth it"? Of course not. But my tears and pain are always mitigated when I kneel in worship before the Lord. Standing awe-struck in God's presence and witnessing him bless others through you will do that to a person.

Proverbs reminds us, "A person's steps are directed by the LORD. How then can anyone understand their own way?" (Prov 20:24 NIV). Indeed, all of life is ruled by the mysterious, providential hand of God. The difficult road we are sometimes forced to travel is never without meaning and purpose. If we are God's children, although it may seem as if his hand is against us, the Lord is always working for our good and his glory.

My prayer is that you will know the joy and peace that comes from walking with Jesus on the Bethlehem Road. And may God work your bitterness for your good and his glory.

---

2. Quoted in David Atkinson, *The Wings of Refuge* (Downers Grove, IL: InterVarsity Press, 1983), 61.

O God, she was a rock of truth;
Ignite in us the faith of Ruth.

JOHN PIPER

ABBREVIATIONS

ABD	*The Anchor Bible Dictionary*. Ed. David Noel Freeman. 6 vols. New York: Doubleday, 1992.
ANE	Ancient Near East(ern)
BASOR	*Bulletin of the American Schools of Oriental Research*
BibInt	*Biblical Interpretation*
CBQ	*Catholic Biblical Quarterly*
ESV	English Standard Version
HCSB	Holman Christian Study Bible
JBL	*Journal of Biblical Literature*
JBQ	*Jewish Bible Quarterly*
JCS	*Journal of Cuneiform Studies*
JNES	*Journal of Near Eastern Studies*
JNSL	*Journal of Northwest Semitic Languages*
JOTT	*Journal of Translation and Textlinguistics*
KJV	King James Version
NASU	New American Standard Bible — Updated Edition
NCV	New Century Version

NIDOTTE	*New International Dictionary of Old Testament Theology and Exegesis.* Ed. Willem A. VanGemeren. 5 vols. Grand Rapids: Zondervan, 1997.
NIV	New International Version
NLT	New Living Translation
NT	New Testament
OT	Old Testament
ResQ	*Restoration Quarterly*
TDOT	*Theological Dictionary of the Old Testament.* Eds. G. J. Botterweck and H. Ringgren. Trans. J. T. Willis, G. W. Bromiley, and D. E. Green. 15 vols. Grand Rapids: Eerdmans, 1974–.
VT	*Vetus Testamentum*
ZAW	*Zeitschrift für die Alttestamentlice Wissenschaft*

ACKNOWLEDGMENTS

To Tim and Pam Ashley. Every time I try to find adequate words to say thank you for the *hesed* you have shown my family, I'm overwhelmed by tears of joy and gratitude and amazement...

To Jeff and Laura Jenkins. In all our heartaches, they have been as faithful as a thousand Ruths. God has used this Christ-glorifying couple in countless ways to make known his magnificent providence.

To Jon Page and Phylicia Gibbs, my co-workers, who have been loyal supporters of the first rank.

To my church family at Carter Lake Road. May you continue to be a wonderful place of refuge for the discouraged and brokenhearted. A million thanks for your love and support. I am not worthy.

To Bill Camp, Cheryl Drennon, Brandon Edwards, Stephen Sutton, and others for their very generous support of this project.

To Paul O'Rear. Thank you for your friendship, your inspiration, and for writing a fantastic *Foreword*.

To my wife. Many generations will rise up and call you blessed (Prov 31:28). May your name echo with all the righteous women in Israel.

To my son. Always remember two things: I will always love you, and you have no reason to fear the Bethlehem Road if the Lord is with you.

To my Kinsman-Redeemer, the Lord Jesus Christ, who transforms our pain to praise. Shelter us beneath your wings until you return...

BIBLIOGRAPHY

Arnold, Bill T., and Bryan E. Beyer. *Encountering the Old Testament*. 2nd ed. Grand Rapids: Baker, 2008.

Block, Daniel I. *Judges, Ruth*. Nashville: B&H, 1999.

Campbell, Edward F., Jr. *Ruth*. Garden City, NY: Doubleday, 1975.

Coffman, James Burton. *Judges and Ruth*. Abilene, TX: ACU Press, 1992.

Driesbach, Jason. "Ruth" in *Cornerstone Biblical Commentary*. Vol. 3. Carol Stream, IL: Tyndale House, 2012.

Eskenazi, Tamara Cohn, and Tikva Frymer-Kensky. *Ruth*. Philadelphia: Jewish Publication Society, 2011.

Fuerst, Wesley J. *The Books of Ruth, Esther, Ecclesiastes, the Song of Songs, Lamentations*. Cambridge: Cambridge Univ. Press, 1975.

Goldingay, John. *Joshua, Judges, and Ruth for Everyone*. Louisville: Westminster John Knox, 2011.

Gray, John. *Joshua, Judges, Ruth*. Grand Rapids: Eerdmans, 1986.

Hamilton, Victor P. *Handbook on the Historical Books*. Grand Rapids: Baker, 2001.

Harrison, R. K. "Ruth" in *Evangelical Commentary on the Bible*. Ed. Walter A. Elwell. Grand Rapids: Baker, 1989.

Hubbard, Robert L. *The Book of Ruth*. Grand Rapids: Eerdmans, 1988.

Jackman, David. *Judges, Ruth*. Dallas: Word, 1991.

Jamieson, Robert, A. R. Fausset, and David Brown. *A Commentary Critical, Experimental and Practical on the Old and New Testament.* Vol. 3. Grand Rapids: Eerdmans, 1948.

LaSor, William Sanford, David Allan Hubbard, and Frederic Wm. Bush. *Old Testament Survey.* Grand Rapids: Eerdmans, 1982.

MacArthur, John F., Jr. *Twelve Extraordinary Women.* Nashville: Nelson, 2005.

—. *The MacArthur Study Bible.* Nashville: Nelson, 1997.

Manor, Dale W. "Ruth" in *Zondervan Illustrated Bible Backgrounds Commentary: Old Testament.* Vol. 2. Grand Rapids: Zondervan, 2009.

Moore, Michael S. "Ruth" in *Joshua, Judges, Ruth.* Grand Rapids: Baker, 2012.

Morris, Leon. "Ruth" in *Judges & Ruth.* Downers Grove, IL: Inter-Varsity Press, 1968.

Nielsen, Kirsten. *Ruth.* Louisville: Westminster John Knox, 1997.

Piper, John. *A Sweet and Bitter Providence.* Wheaton, IL: Crossway, 2010.

Sakenfeld, Katherine Doob. *Ruth.* Louisville: John Knox, 1999.

Smith, James E. *The Books of History.* Joplin, MO: College Press, 1995.

Walton, John H., Victor H. Matthews, and Mark W. Chavalas. *The IVP Bible Background Commentary: Old Testament.* Downers Grove, IL: InterVarsity Press, 2000.

Webb, Barry G. *Five Festal Garments.* Downers Grove, IL: InterVarsity Press, 2000.

Wiersbe, Warren. *Be Committed.* Wheaton, IL: Victor, 1993.

Younger, K. Lawson, Jr. *Judges and Ruth.* Grand Rapids: Zondervan, 2002.

ὥσπερ ξένοι χαίρουσι πατρίδα βλέπειν
οὕτως καὶ τοῖς κάμνουσι βιβλίου τέλος